McSweeney's

THE McSWEENEY'S BOOK OF POLITICS AND MUSICALS

McSweeney's is a publishing company based in San Francisco. As well as running the daily humor website *McSweeney's Internet Tendency*, McSweeney's publishes *McSweeney's Quarterly Concern*, *The Believer*, *Lucky Peach*, *Wholphin*, *Grantland Quarterly*, and an ever-growing selection of books under various imprints.

ALSO FROM McSWEENEY'S

THE McSWEENEY'S BOOK OF POLITICS AND MUSICALS

THE McSWEENEY'S BOOK OF POLITICS AND MUSICALS

Edited by Christopher Monks of
McSweeney's Internet Tendency

VINTAGE BOOKS
A Division of Random House, Inc.
New York

A VINTAGE BOOKS ORIGINAL, JULY 2012

Copyright © 2012 by McSweeney's Publishing LLC

All rights reserved. Published in the United States by Vintage Books,
a division of Random House, Inc., New York, and in Canada by
Random House of Canada Limited, Toronto.

Vintage and colophon are registered trademarks of Random House, Inc.

"Fragments from *BAILOUT! THE MUSICAL*" first appeared on *The New Yorker*
online.

Some of these selections were first published on McSweeneys.net. All selections are
copyright to the contributors.

Library of Congress Cataloging-in-Publication Data
The McSweeney's book of politics and musicals.
p. cm.
ISBN 978-0-307-38734-9 (pbk.)
1. American wit and humor.
2. United States—Politics and government—Humor. I. McSweeney's.
PN6231.P6M37 2012
818'.60208—dc23
2012013819

Cover concept and design by Brian McMullen and his son Alton. (That's them in the photo.)
Photograph by Jason Fulford

www.vintagebooks.com

Printed in the United States of America
10 9 8 7 6 5 4 3 2 1

CONTENTS

FOREWORD

Wyatt Cenac

If you are reading this, it means that someone just gave you this book as a gift. Congratulations. Whatever you did was more than likely "gift-worthy." You probably had a birthday or a half birthday. Maybe you graduated from an institution of higher learning or you escaped from prison. Or your significant other gave you this book to keep you quiet on a road trip to Oakland. In any case, you accomplished something impressive enough that someone felt this book would be the perfect thing that would speak to your sensibilities, amuse you, and keep you quiet on the 580 freeway. If you bought this book for yourself, then sincerest apologies that nobody likes you enough to buy it for you. But don't give up hope.

Not the hope that you will be more likeable. That is out of this book's hands because there may be real reasons why nobody should like you. Reasons that can't be found in the pages of this book. Still read this book, but afterwards find yourself a nice self-help book, like *McSweeney's Book of Self-Improvement, Actualization, and Musicals*, which will be in bookstores next never. But putting that aside, the point is don't give up hope in its most general sense. It is a truly American ideal. Apple pie is almost as American as hope. Or so it hopes.

It was hope that brought the first colonists to this country in search of a better land that would allow them social and religious freedoms that they could then deny others. It was hope that put smallpox in blankets, thereby making this land a bit cheaper to purchase from its original owners. Hope put tea in a harbor, angering and confusing the British as well as today's senior citizens. Hope gave sciatica to a black lady on a bus in Montgomery, inspiring a civil rights movement while encouraging the health benefits of walking at least thirty minutes a day. Hope keeps same-sex partners together, looking toward the day when they, too, can legally get divorced.

Hope is the binding agent for political discourse in the United States. As a voter, one hopes their needs are being listened to and addressed. As a politician, one hopes their message gets out while their indiscretions with flight attendants stay hidden, along with that secret love child they had with a wolf. As a political humorist, one hopes that no matter how troubling times may seem from moment to moment, people will always be able to find laughter in the situation. And as a manager of a coffee shop in Brooklyn, one hopes that times will never be so troubled that the political humorist you once foolishly employed as a barista will return looking for their old job again.

Obviously, there is more to the American democratic system than just those four individuals. You also have the media, the lobbyists, the protest groups, the unions, the action committees, the think tanks, the activists, the foreign business partners, the intergalactic business partners, the special-interest groups, the skeptics, the financial donors, the blood donors, the senior citizens, the public sector, the private sector, the Nigerian princes, the bureaucrats, the steering committees, Main Street, Wall Street, and ghosts. All with their own needs and the hope that their voices will drown out yours. And for the right price, it can.

For as wonderful as America is, it is a country where we still make people vote in November to accommodate farmers from a hundred and fifty years ago who probably still won't make it to the polls in time because they are either dead or vampires. *Vampire Farm*: coming to the CW next fall.

It runs on a political system whose parties are represented by animals that tend to stink up barns and circuses and usually spend most of their time swatting away the filthy gnats that are attracted to them. The same is true of politicians. The floors of the Capitol Building get hosed down every night to keep the senators from getting hoof and mouth.

It's a place where the state of Texas is at the bottom of high-school graduation rates, but gets to dictate what goes into the country's textbooks because the other forty-nine states need its delicious chili recipes. If you are reading this and you graduated from a school in Texas—good job. Next time, try it without sounding the words out loud.

It's a country where people are scared to sit next to a Muslim on an airplane, but have no problem if that Muslim drives them home from the airport . . . so long as he avoids the Midtown Tunnel. If you're reading this while in a cab, don't look up! They're probably watching you.

It's a country where a football team with a mascot of a Native American man could play a team whose mascot is a colonial soldier in the Super Bowl, and even if they won, afterward they'd still be called the Redskins.

But for all of the problems in this country, it's still a country that people love for its hope. It is the hope that we can strive to be better as individuals and as a whole, and, if not, then we can at least afford to import better individuals who will in turn inspire us to be better or marry us for green cards.

One of the things that makes this country great is the ability to learn from our mistakes, laugh at them, publish them on the Internet, and then collect them in book form to be sold to rubes. Not you. The person who bought it for you.

This book is filled with some of *McSweeney's Internet Tendency's* finest humor from both regular contributors and guest contributors who decided to slum it in the land of the written word.

And it is my hope that you find this book funny. I haven't read it. I'm waiting for someone to gift it to me. I hope I'll enjoy it.

THE McSWEENEY'S
BOOK OF POLITICS AND
MUSICALS

MY AMERICA: A NEW ACTION MOVIE SCREENPLAY BY SARAH PALIN

Wendy Molyneux

FADE IN:

INT. THE WASHINGTON MONUMENT (1776)

George Washington and Betsy Ross are sitting in the living room of their house, which is inside the Washington Monument.

George is oiling his chest by the light of a crackling fire. Betsy is working on a prototype of the Confederate Flag.

GEORGE

I have a bad feeling about tonight, Betsy. A bad feeling.

BETSY

Oh, George, you are always saying that. That's one of the things I love about you so much.

They kiss. They are married.

GEORGE

I am so glad I divorced Martha and married you instead.

BETSY

There is no shame in quitting something in the middle because it is not working and because your NATION needs you.

GEORGE

Agreed.

They shake hands.

Suddenly, there is a BIG FLASH of smoke and a KNOCK on the door. Betsy opens it, and it is Abraham Lincoln.

BETSY

Who are you?

ABRAHAM LINCOLN

It is me, Abraham Lincoln, and I am FROM THE FUTURE.

GEORGE

The future? My God.

ABRAHAM LINCOLN

It's your God I am worried about. And your taxes and freedoms.

BETSY

Please come in and sit down and tell us.

ABRAHAM LINCOLN

There is no time. Everyone is in grave danger. Let's get in my time machine and I'll tell you as we travel.

GEORGE WASHINGTON
Where are we going?

ABRAHAM LINCOLN
(looks serious)
2012.

A bunch of music plays.

INT. TIME MACHINE

They have all gotten in the time machine, which is super-nice, with plush mahogany chairs, a bar, and a flight attendant who caters to their every whim.

BETSY ROSS
Okay, now tell us what in the Sam Hill is going on.

ABRAHAM LINCOLN
In the year 2012, the Russians and Muslims are attacking the U.S. under the leadership of one very bad man who is like Hitler, Barack Obama.

GEORGE WASHINGTON
Who's Hitler?

ABRAHAM LINCOLN
That's not important right now. What's important is that the Russians and Muslims are invading America. Through Alaska.

GEORGE WASHINGTON
Oh, no. Not Alaska.

ABRAHAM LINCOLN

Yes. Alaska. They have strapped nuclear bombs to wolves and moose, and are sending them down to America.

BETSY ROSS

What can we do?

ABRAHAM LINCOLN

We can fight.

EXT. ALASKA WILDERNESS – LATER

George Washington, Abraham Lincoln, and Betsy Ross get off the time machine. They are refreshed from the in-flight service, but also ready for battle, and they have guns. BIG ONES.

BETSY ROSS

Tell us more about this Barack Obama. How will we know him when we see him?

ABRAHAM LINCOLN

Because he is like Hitler.

GEORGE WASHINGTON

From what you told us in the time machine, maybe we should go kill Hitler first and then come back and get this guy.

ABE punches GEORGE in the face.

ABRAHAM LINCOLN

No! You don't get it. Our values are under attack.

GEORGE WASHINGTON

(rubbing his jaw)
Thanks, I needed that.

BETSY ROSS

You two boys stop fighting. We have some moose and wolves to kill.

BEAUTIFUL VOICE (O.S.)

Darn right we do.

The voice steps out of the woods and it belongs to a very BEAUTIFUL WOMAN named Sara Pallon (not Sarah Palin).

GEORGE

Who are you?

BEAUTIFUL VOICE (SARA)

I am Sara Pallon. I was the governor of this state until I quit to do a secret job for the government, researching these Muslims undercover for years while pretending to just be an ordinary beautiful public figure.

ABRAHAM LINCOLN

Whoa.

BEAUTIFUL SARA PALLON

Yeah. Now let's stop talking and get in my helicopter.

She pulls aside a bush, revealing a state-of-the-art helicopter with gorgeous teak furniture inside. A flight attendant welcomes them aboard.

INT. HELICOPTER

SARA PALLON

Yippee-kay-yay, motherfuckers.

The helicopter zooms over the sky.

They look out the windows and see an ARMY OF WOLVES, MOOSE, AND BEARS with nuclear bombs all strapped to them.

In front, riding on a motorcycle, is BARACK OBAMA.

SARA PALLON

Grab your guns. Let's shoot some animals.

Betsy Ross, Abe, and George all grab their guns. (Sara taught them how to use them in the helicopter.)

They all shoot the nuclear animals and then they land in front of Barack Obama.

They get off the helicopter.

SARA PALLON

Looks like this is the end of the line for you, Barack Obama.

BARACK OBAMA

You are right. I have seen the error of my ways, and I am making you president.

He takes off his crown and puts it on Sara Pallon.

Everyone is crying by now.

ABRAHAM LINCOLN

Before I go, I just want to say one thing.

He gets down on one knee.

SARA PALLON

Go ahead and say it, Mr. Lincoln.

ABRAHAM LINCOLN

I love you.

SARA PALLON

Me, too.

FADE OUT:

EPILOGUE

Sara Pallon and Abraham Lincoln are making love. She looks great.

THE END

PRESIDENTIAL STATS

Simon Rich

One thing I'm interested in is how many U.S. presidents have murdered people. I don't care about how many have "caused deaths," by ordering bombings or declaring wars or allowing poverty or whatever. The thing I want to know is: How many of them have actually picked up a murder weapon and killed someone? How many presidents have sharpened a knife and plunged it into another man's throat? Or blown someone's legs off with a rocket, or fired a cannonball into somebody's screaming face? How many U.S. presidents have actually, physically, murdered people?

In order to answer this question, I did research for an hour on Wikipedia. Here is what I found out. Of the forty-four U.S. presidents, thirteen (30 percent) have probably murdered people. There are also six other presidents who might have murdered people, but I can't really tell. The rest probably didn't kill anyone.

Here is a list of all the presidents and what I could figure out about them.

George Washington
Did he murder anyone? Yes.

Who? Some French people and some Indians.

When? During the French and Indian War, when he was in his early twenties.

How'd he do it? Washington used a curved steel sword to murder people. The sword was thirty-six inches long, the size of a large high-school baseball bat. Because Washington was a lieutenant colonel in the British army, he probably murdered people while riding around on a horse. He was six foot two—and his horse, Nelson, was at least five feet tall. So in order to murder people, he had to swing his sword down into their necks as he rode past them. There's no way to know for sure, but it's possible that he cut some people's heads all the way off.

John Adams
Did he murder anyone? No.

Thomas Jefferson
Did he murder anyone? No.

James Madison
Did he murder anyone? Possibly.

Who? Some British people.

When? During the American Revolution, when he was about twenty-five.

How'd he do it? Madison was a colonel, so if he murdered anyone, he probably did it while riding around on a horse, Washington-style.

James Monroe
Did he murder anyone? Yes.

Who? British people.

When? During the American Revolution, when he was a teenager.

How'd he do it? Monroe murdered people with a musket/bayonet combo. He ran around with it all day, stabbing people in the heart and shooting them in the face.

John Quincy Adams

Did he murder anyone? No.

Andrew Jackson

Did he murder anyone? Yes.

Who? British people, Indians, some Canadians, and a guy named Charles Dickinson.

When? In a duel and some wars.

How'd he do it? In 1808, he shot Charles Dickinson in the heart with a pistol. He fired the gun from twenty-four feet away, which is about the distance of an NBA three-pointer, if you're shooting from the top of the key. The men were dueling over an argument they had had a few months earlier about horse racing. Jackson knew Dickinson was a faster draw, and he didn't try to beat him to the first shot. Instead, he stood still and allowed Dickinson to fire first. Dickinson shot him in the ribs. Jackson hesitated for a while, clutching his chest. Then, he slowly aimed his gun at Dickinson and murdered him.

Later on, in the Creek War, Jackson used pistols, muskets, and cannons to murder Indians.

Martin Van Buren

Did he murder anyone? No.

William Henry Harrison

Did he murder anyone? Yes.

Who? Some Indians.

When? In the Battle of Fallen Timbers, when he was eighteen.

How'd he do it? Probably by shooting them in the face.

John Tyler

Did he murder anyone? Maybe.

Who? British people, possibly, or some Indians.

When? In the War of 1812, when he was in his early twenties.

How? Rifles, swords.

James K. Polk
Murder anyone? No. Polk was a colonel in a militia cavalry regiment, so he knew how to murder people, but he never actually murdered anyone.

Zachary Taylor
Murder people? Yes.
    Who? Indians.
    When? In 1812, when he was in his late twenties. I assume he shot them in the face.

Millard Fillmore
No.

Franklin Pierce
Maybe.
    Who? Some Mexican people.
    When? In the Mexican-American War, when he was forty-three. Pierce was pretty old when he volunteered for this war and had already served as a congressman, so he probably didn't actually have to murder anyone. It's possible.

James Buchanan
Probably.
    Who? Some British people.
    When? While serving in the War of 1812, in his early twenties.
    How? With a rifle.

Abraham Lincoln
No. Although he was a captain in the Black Hawk War, and was trained to murder Indians, he didn't actually murder any.

Andrew Johnson
No.

Ulysses S. Grant

Yes.

Who? Mexicans.

When? In over half a dozen battles during the Mexican-American War.

How? As a young, low-ranking officer, Grant had to engage in hand-to-hand musket and bayonet combat. This means that he probably shot people in the face from very close range or slit their throats open with a sword so their blood would gush out and they would die. He was promoted twice for bravery.

Rutherford B. Hayes

Yes.

Who? Southerners.

When? During the Civil War, when he was forty.

How'd he do it? Hayes shot people in the face with a musket and stabbed them in the heart with a bayonet, sometimes while riding on a horse and sometimes while running around on the ground. He fought for four years.

James Garfield

Yes.

Who? Southerners.

When? During the Civil War, when he was in his early thirties.

How? Garfield was in charge of cavalry, so he definitely killed people while riding on a horse.

Chester A. Arthur

No.

Grover Cleveland

No.

Benjamin Harrison
Probably not. He served as a brigadier general in the Civil War, but generals usually don't murder anyone themselves.

William McKinley
Yes.

    Who? Some people from Virginia.

    When? At the start of the Civil War, when he was a teenager.

    How? As a young private, McKinley probably murdered people with one of those musket/bayonet things, by slicing their stomachs open or shooting bullets into their chests.

Theodore Roosevelt
Yes.

    Who? Some Spanish people.

    When? During the Spanish-American War.

    How? With a revolver. He probably shot them in the face.

Taft, Wilson, Harding, Coolidge, Hoover, and **Franklin D. Roosevelt** didn't murder anyone.

Harry S. Truman might have murdered some Europeans while serving in World War I, but probably not.

Dwight D. Eisenhower never saw combat and probably didn't murder anyone.

JFK might have killed people in World War II from very far away.

Lyndon B. Johnson and **Richard M. Nixon** served in World War II, but neither of them killed anyone.

Gerald R. Ford killed some people in World War II in the South

Pacific, by blowing up their boats with torpedoes so they would burn to death or drown. He also might have shot some planes out of the sky, causing people to explode in midair or fall thousands of feet to their deaths.

Carter and **Reagan** didn't kill anyone.

George H. W. Bush killed people in World War II when he was a teenager, by bombing their ships so they drowned.

Bill Clinton, **George W. Bush**, and **Barack Obama** have not killed anyone.

FROM THE DIARY OF JOHN ADAMS

Peter Krinke

July 3, 1776

Tomorrow the Congress shall vote on wording for the Declaration of our Independence from England. While I shall endorse its passage, I cannot deny my contempt for its author, the foul Virginian Thomas Jefferson.

Today, as the Congress was being called to order, I was heard to remark that I have come to the conclusion that one useless man is a shame, two is a law firm, and three or more is a congress. While Delegate Cushing struggled at breath for his chortling, Delegate Jefferson closed his eyes, cocked his head askew (pretending to rest it upon a "pillow" of his hands), and proceeded to snore loudly.

"Dear Sir," I responded, hoping to restore a modicum of dignity to the proceedings, "becalm yourself."

Jefferson, in what initially seemed an attempt at reconciliation, apologized and told me he'd actually commissioned a large run of my *Thoughts on Government* from a local printer. He informed me that they were of service to a great number of the Congress.

He then extended his hand to me, and, mollified by his contrite demeanor, I reached to shake it. But at the last moment, he jerked his hand away and adjusted his wig, running his hand along the side of it!

Jefferson then called a number of the other delegates over and pretended to study me intently, with and without the aid of Benjamin Franklin's spectacles, while asking in jest, "Is that Benedict Arnold, or is that John Adams?"

"'Tis I, John Adams!" I retorted.

In response, Jefferson informed the Congress he was going to pretend to be someone else for their amusement. He then produced a lace handkerchief from his pocket and, holding it between his thumb and forefinger, his wrist cocked at a ninety-degree angle, began prancing about in the manner of a fop or dandy, proclaiming, "I'm John Adams! I favor a strong federal government to the detriment of states' rights and the sovereignty of the individual."

"I demand you cease these unflattering characterizations of me," I cried.

Resolving to fight fire with fire, I called over the delegation from the Province of New Hampshire and proclaimed loudly, "I, too, would like to slander and ridicule a fellow delegate through a keen approximation of his physical characteristics and mannerisms."

Then, hunching over and placing a finger in my nose while adopting the tone and register of Jefferson's peculiar Virginian vocal timbre, I proclaimed, "I'm Tom-E Jefferson! The delegate from Virgin-*I*-a!"

While the majority of the Congress looked away from my ill-advised impersonation, Jefferson began to clap loudly, pretending to congratulate me.

Feigning enthusiasm for my performance, he slapped me on the back, proclaiming, "An excellent likeness!" Then, turning to the Congress and placing his hand next to his mouth in order to shield his words from me, but still speaking with a volume intended to be audible to everyone present, he continued, "It was as if your mother were in the room with us, dressed in your clothing."

"How dare you?" I screamed. "My mother is dead."

Jefferson looked genuinely surprised and, turning again to

address the Congress, proclaimed, "She seemed animated enough last night!"

So filled with rage was I that I retired to the lavatory in order to regain my composure. Upon entering the privy I noticed a stack of my *Thoughts on Government* resting next to the seat, with a sign beside it in Jefferson's hand, penned, "Not for reading!" and an arrow pointing to my texts!

On several occasions Delegate Jefferson has smelled of hemp and mead before the noon meal. He also frequently takes leave to an antechamber with his servant Sally Hemings, proclaiming they are off to "a different kind of congress." He says this while winking!

When pressed as to the infrequency of his visits to the bedchamber of his wife, Jefferson recites the crude maxim, "Once a quill is dipped in black ink, it forever favors that hue."

But enough of Jefferson and his clownish antics; I must rest. Tomorrow I shall help birth a republic.

Ah, what's this? I hear a knock upon my door! And quick footfalls! What could it be? A gift from an admirer? A note of great import? I'll just have a quick look . . .

Indignity! The indignity of indignities!

Upon opening the door, I observed a sack upon my stoop, and it was aflame! I quickly moved to smother the inferno by stomping upon it soundly, only to discover the contents: horse void! From a sick horse!

As I recoiled in horror from my investigative sniff, the sound of Jefferson and his cohorts' cackles resounded down the cobblestone streets.

My only solace comes from my steely belief in the providential certainty that history will reveal Jefferson as the base and immoral cad he truly is.

AN ANTI-WASHINGTON CANDIDATE'S STUMP SPEECH

Pete Reynolds

Good afternoon, my fellow Americans. Our nation is in a time of crisis. Unemployment is high. Home values are low. And the folks in Washington would have you believe that they can solve all your problems. But we know better. We know that Washington, D.C., doesn't have the solutions.

Now, I'm not from Washington, D.C. No one can say I'm part of the Washington establishment. You won't find me at a Washington, D.C., cocktail party, laughing and wife-swapping on the taxpayer's dime while the economy crumbles. No, sir. I've never even been to Washington, D.C.. Actually, I'd go so far as to say that I literally could not even find Washington, D.C., on a map, and not because I don't know how to use a map.

My friends, I've never even heard of Washington, D.C. I do not even believe in the concept of Washington, D.C. And as I stand here before you today, I can promise you that Washington, D.C., is not even a term I understand as a proper noun. Frankly, it sounds made up.

In truth, I am a complete stranger to Washington, D.C. If I were to drive up in a windowless van and offer candy to Washington, D.C., Washington, D.C., would be wise to reject my offer. Even if I told Washington, D.C., that its mom was running late and sent me to pick it up after school—and even if I somehow correctly guessed the family password—Washington, D.C., should still not get into my van. That is how much of a stranger I am to Washington, D.C. If Washington, D.C., actually did make the grievous error of getting into my van, I would disregard the ensuing AMBER Alert, because I would not even understand that Washington, D.C., could be missing. This hypothetical has now turned in on itself.

Just as Washington, D.C., should not trust me, I, in turn, do not trust Washington, D.C. I would not allow Washington, D.C., to house-sit, for example. If I did, I would not expect Washington, D.C., to water my plants, even if Washington, D.C., made multiple promises to do so.

Washington, D.C.? More like "Someplace I'm not part of the elite of, D.C."

I do not understand this world as being capable of containing anything called Washington, D.C. I believe Washington, D.C., to be one giant hologram. Washington, D.C., like my gay son, is dead to me.

In closing, I'd like to share with you a conversation I had with my six-year-old granddaughter just the other day that I think pretty much sums it up. She asked me, "Grandpa, why aren't the empty suits in Washington, D.C., doing anything to help regular folks like us?" And do you know what I told her? I said, "Sweetheart, what the hell is a 'Washington, D.C.'?"

I'm asking for your vote on November sixth. Reelect me, and I promise to keep on doing what I've been doing for the last twelve years: working hard to represent you, the people, in Congress, wherever that is.

MY 1-1-1-1-1-1-1 PLAN

Ellie Kemper

The time has come to stop kidding ourselves, and to start being serious with ourselves. Freedom can only thrive in a nation that doesn't kill freedom. I, for one, am very interested in living in a living-freedom nation. And I would like to invite you to join me.

My 1-1-1-1-1-1-1 Plan works as follows:

1 Chef in the Kitchen

Have you ever heard the phrase "too many cooks spoil the broth"? This really applies to what I'm talking about. Too many chefs in the White House kitchen not only ruin soups, but also cost you—the taxpayer—hundreds more dollars every year. Think of that, and then tell me you wouldn't prefer just one chef cooking meals for me (and my family) in the kitchen. Bon appétit, America.

1 Teacher for Every 10 to 50 or so Students

America is falling behind in education. I, for example, was never once asked to diagram a sentence in all my years at school. Classes are too big, and not every student is getting the attention she deserves. Under my plan, every ten to between fifty and seventy-five students will be provided with *their own* teacher, for the duration of the class, whether it is just one subject, study hall, or an entire day of teaching all the subjects. Nailing down precise class size is difficult at this point, because you never know when people are moving, switching school districts, getting expelled, etc. But read my lips: no more than ninety (or so) students per one teacher.

1 9% Business Flat Tax–9% Individual Flat Tax–9% National Sales Tax Combo

I think (hope) this will work.

1 More Day Off During Christmas Vacation

Christmas Vacation, Holiday Hiatus, Winter Acknowledgment, whatever you want to call it: we all could use an extra day to relax. What exactly is the problem? Under my watch, you would be able to enjoy that extra day to travel back from St. Maarten, or that extra morning to sleep in after the out-of-towners have left, or those extra hours to get the last of your thank-you notes in the mail. And to those of you with kids who ask, "How are we supposed to get that done if our kids are home and not at school? Who exactly is supposed to take care of them?" I would like to answer: What do you do every Saturday? Figure it out, America. I know you can.

1 Free Health Benefit Given to Every American in Good Health

Like the great man who started this all, I cannot tell a lie: I am not fully up to date on what the current status of health reform is. Did they pass that bill? What exactly is happening with that bill? It doesn't really matter. The truth is our government helps those who help themselves. Never before has there been such a strong incentive to shed those extra five pounds, to make sure that you are taking the stairs instead of the elevator, and to hold off on going to the hospital and instead just wait that abdominal pain out. These free benefits will be doled out in a "mystery meat" fashion, which is to say that you won't know the exact benefit until you actually earn it. What we can tell you is that the size of the health benefit will be directly linked to the size of your commitment to good health. Supersize that commitment, America.

1 Free Ford Fiesta for Every Citizen Who Votes for Me

This offer is subject to availability/willingness of the Ford Motor Company, which—as of this date of the unveiling of my 1-1-1-1-1-1-1 Plan—has not been returning my calls.

1 Chance to Show Your Citizenship Card, and If You Can't, Then You're Out

A lot of immigrants mean well, but they are illegal. And they are taking our jobs, our health care dollars, and our babies in the dead of night. America can no longer afford to be polite to everyone who wants in. It is time to ask suspicious-looking individuals for their citizenship cards, and if they can't produce one, then we will figure out what to do with them from there.

In closing, my 1-1-1-1-1-1-1 Plan will get America out of the gutter and onto the sidewalk. That sidewalk will then lead to the Castle of Liberty, where all Americans will live together. The gutter, mean-while, will be repaved in gold, and then made into a part of the side-walk. Come and walk this sidewalk with me, America.

WHERE IS THE REST OF THIS GRAPH?

Ben Greenman

DOWN THERE

UP THERE

THE ONLY THING THAT CAN STOP THIS ASTEROID IS YOUR LIBERAL ARTS DEGREE

Mike Lacher

By now you're probably wondering what this is all about, why FBI agents pulled you out of your barista job, threw you on a helicopter, and brought you to NASA headquarters. There's no time, so I'll shoot it to you straight. You've seen the news reports. What hit New York wasn't some debris from an old satellite.

There's an asteroid the size of Montana heading toward Earth, and if it hits us, the planet is over. But we've got one last-ditch plan. We need a team to land on the surface of the asteroid, drill a nuclear warhead one mile into its core, and get out before it explodes. And you're just the liberal arts major we need to lead that team.

Sure, we've got dozens of astronauts, physicists, and demolitions experts. I'll be damned if we didn't try to train our best men for this mission. But just because they can fly a shuttle and understand higher-level astrophysics doesn't mean they can execute a unique mission like this. Anyone can learn how to land a spacecraft on a rocky asteroid flying through space at twelve miles per second. I don't need some pencilneck with four PhDs, one thousand hours of simulator time, and the ability to operate a robot crane in low-Earth orbit. I need someone with four years of broad-but-humanities-focused studies, three subsequent years in temp jobs, and the ability to reason across multiple areas of study. I need someone who can read *The Bell Jar* and make strong observations about its representations of mental health and the repression of women. Sure, you've never even flown a plane before, but with only ten days until the asteroid hits, there's no one better to nuke the thing.

I've seen your work, and it's damn impressive. Your midterm paper on the semiotics of *Band of Outsiders* turned a lot of heads at mission control. Your performance in Biology For Non-Science Majors was impressive, matched only by your mastery of second-year Portuguese. And a lot of the research we do here couldn't have happened without your groundbreaking work on suburban malaise and its representation and repression in John Hughes's films. I hope you're still that good, because when you're lowering a hydrogen bomb into a craggy mass of flying astronomic death with barely any gravity, you're going to need to draw on all the multidisciplinary reason and analysis you've got.

Don't think I don't have my misgivings about sending some hotshot Asian Studies minor into space for the first time. This is NASA, not Grinnell. I don't have the time or patience for your renegade attitude and macho bravado. I can't believe the fate of mankind rests on some roughneck bachelor of the arts. I know your type. You feed off the thrill of inference and small, instructor-led discussions. You think you're some kind of invincible god just because you have cursory understandings of Buddhism, classical literature, and introductory linguistics. Well, listen up, cowboy. You make one false move up there, be it a clumsy thesis statement, poorly reasoned argument, or glib analysis, and your team is dead, along with this whole sorry planet.

I've wasted enough time with chatter. Let's get you over to mission control. Our avionics team needs your help getting their paper on gender politics in *The Matrix* properly cited in MLA format.

DEBATE FOR EMPEROR OF THE UPSILON SIGMA STAR SYSTEM

Teddy Wayne

MODERATOR: Welcome back to Quarzon University and the debate for emperor of the Upsilon Sigma star system between Senator Demoq the Populist and High Council Elder Gopox the Compassionate. A hot topic is wormhole transformation. Which of you doesn't believe in the theory? Can I see a show of tentacles?

DEMOQ: I'm amazed we're still debating wormhole transformation in the year 12,535 After Dorzon.

GOPOX: Let me clarify. Although I *do* believe in wormhole transformation, when I gaze outside my starship with my seven eyes at the Valporian sun shining on the Paronius Galaxy, I see the Divine Creator Dorzon's residual trail of slime.

MODERATOR: Indeed, a beautiful image. Let's turn to the economy. Demoq, financial stratification has been a central plank of your campaign.

DEMOQ: I believe we now have two Upsilon Sigmas: the oxygen-rich and the oxygen-poor.

GOPOX: How can Demoq claim any authority on this subject when he owns an opulent twenty-two-moon planet and spent four hundred zazoos on a cranial epidermis replacement?

DEMOQ: Yet you're allowed to dodge the starfleet draft and vote for the Iota-12 War? You're nothing but a chicken-clone-hawk-clone!

MODERATOR: Please restrain yourselves from making ad alienum attacks. Demoq, are you fully against the war?

DEMOQ: While I don't rule out interstellar combat in all cases, I believe we were duped into fighting this mismanaged star war for scientifically fictional reasons, and it is time to teleport our troops home. It's distracting us from other priorities, such as universal health insurance.

GOPOX: It is not the responsibility of the Upsilon Sigma government to provide health care to the *entire* universe. And if we leave Iota-12 now, then the space pirates from 942.8/15.6 have already won.

DEMOQ: The tragic events of 942.8/15.6 were perpetrated by space pirates from the Iota-13 star—Iota-12 had nothing to do with it, and now their inhabitants and the intergalactic community regard us as oppressive colonizers. We've gotten sucked into an unwinnable black hole, and our brave starfighters—whom I support, by the way—are dying in vain for xycanthium deposits. No more green circulatory fluid for xycanthium!

MODERATOR: What do you propose?

DEMOQ: We need to curb our dependence on foreign reserves of xycanthium by doing things like not flying sport-utility mother-ships that get under ten parsecs a gallon—to prevent wars like this *and* to stop the scourge of cosmic warming. We owe it not only to ourselves but also to our larvae and our larvae's larvae.

GOPOX: Great, and while we're setting our mothership industry back countless light-years, why don't we outsource all work to a rival solar system? Or would you rather just take down the planetary force fields and hire the illegal aliens?

DEMOQ: By "illegal aliens," do you mean aliens from other solar systems who live here without citizenship, or do you mean our own alien citizens who act illegally—in other words, criminals?

MODERATOR: We're getting lost in spacial semantics. Last topic: the High Council has been hearing sounds lately of aggression from yet another star system. Should we preemptively invade Earth?

DEMOQ: No—it's another unnecessary war.

GOPOX: This is one area where we agree. Without our intervention, the pitiful Earthlings will soon enough destroy themselves.

MODERATOR: I'm glad we could end on a note of unity and optimism. Tune in next time, when the candidates debate laser control, Homeplanet Security, and interspecies marriage.

VOTE YES ON SPLOST 5

Lucas Klauss

Attention, Hardin City Voter! On your ballot this November, please vote yes on SPLOST (Special-Purpose Local-Option Sales Tax) 5. This temporary, 1 percent tax will fund real improvements to our community, including:

- The demolition of the Tanner Road Skatepark.
- The demolition of the Hardin City Aquatic Complex.
- The demolition of the Rory B. Covel Senior Center.

All of the above were funded and built under SPLOST 4, or, as it has become widely known, "SPLOST Opportunity." These projects were wasteful boondoggles initiated by the previous administration as favors to their well-connected friends. SPLOST 5 is a chance to put such corruption behind us, with exciting upgrades to our city, including:

- The construction of the Tanner Road Skatecenter.
- The construction of the Hardin City Aquatic Park.
- The construction of the Rory B. Covel Senior Complex.

SPLOST 5 is also a chance to revive worthy projects begun under SPLOST 3 but discontinued, damaged, or destroyed under the shortsighted, poorly planned, and (many say) malicious SPLOST 4. Among these ventures are:

- The Lakeside Medical Development, currently under the waters of the Lakeside Lake Development.
- The reinstatement of the Gun Buyback Program and impounding of funds from the Gun Sellback Program.
- The Dr. Ellen Tuttinger Botanical Gardens, which were set aflame by a team from the Dr. Kenneth Nelling Arson Research Group.

Furthermore, SPLOST 5 will provide the community with tools necessary to resolve some of Hardin City's longest-standing challenges, many of which were instigated by SPLOST 2. This "SPLOSTlectric Boogaloo" was, as you may recall, implemented by those later responsible for the "SPLOST Opportunity." Ongoing challenges include:

- Finding a permanent location for the Hardin City Cemetery. Currently it stands on the north side of the city, an area much less suitable than its previous southerly location, but equally as unwelcome as its earlier westerly location, and yet significantly worse than its original easterly location (technically a relocation funded by "The SPLOSTriginal" SPLOST 1). Planners are now investigating ideal spots to the northwest and southeast of the city.
- Finally completing the Piney Lane Over-and-Under-and-Out-and-Around-and-Down-Pass.
- Guaranteeing that the highly suspected waste and fraud of SPLOSTs 2 and 4 are fully investigated and that those responsible serve the longest possible prison terms in the Norwood Valley Prison.
- Building the Norwood Valley Prison.
- Buying a trailer for the middle school.

SPLOST 5 will also amend the Hardin City constitution to say that all future SPLOSTs must be approved by the SPLOST Board, members of which shall be appointed for life by the current administration.

So vote Yes on SPLOST 5, "SPLOSTin' Alive." Let's improve Hardin City—once and for all.

BARACK OBAMA'S UNDERSOLD 2012 CAMPAIGN SLOGANS

Nathaniel Lozier

We Might Be Able To
We're Open to Suggestions
If We Do, We'll Let You Know
I'd Like to See You Try
I Wouldn't Get Your Hopes Up
There Are Only So Many Hours in a Day
Worrying Isn't Going to Solve Anything
We Had Good Intentions
For the Record, We Really Thought We Could Have
It Turns Out We Actually Can't

A COMPREHENSIVE LIST OF THIRD-PLACE FINISHERS FOR U.S. PRESIDENT, 2008–2036

David Warnke

2008: Ralph Nader
2012: Ralph Nader
2016: Ralph Nader
2020: Ralph Nader
2024: Ralph Nader
2028: Ralph Nader
2032: Ralph Nader
2036: Darth Vader

THE LESSER-KNOWN SLOGANS OF POLITICAL MODERATES

Kate Johansen and Katie Bukowski

Live Free or Give Me a Reasonable Alternative!

Peace Through Pragmatism

Let's All Keep Our Opinions to Ourselves for a While!

It's Noontime in America

Some Taxation, Some Representation

What Do We Want? Rational Discussion! When Do We Want It? . . . What Works for You?

Hooray for Prudence!

We Request Change in a Reasonable Amount of Time After Comprehensive Discussion of the Options!

Who Wants Peanuts?

THREE TIMELINES OF THE AMERICAN FINANCIAL MELTDOWN TOLD THROUGH R. L. STINE BOOK TITLES

Matthew Gillespie

From Bust to Bailout (or, *Escape from the Carnival of Horrors*)

Calling All Creeps!
Jerks-in-Training
Under the Magician's Spell
Ghouls Gone Wild
Instant Millionaire
Let's Party!
Be Careful What You Wish For
House of Whispers
Forbidden Secrets
In Too Deep
Are You Terrified Yet?
No Answer
Deep Trouble
Into the Twister of Terror
Into the Jaws of Doom
Last Chance
Dead End

A Shocker on Shock Street
The Hand of Power
Escape from HorrorLand
All-Night Party
The Evil Lives!

The Poor Get Poorer (or, *All-Day Nightmare*)

Children of Fear
Daughters of Silence
Losers in Space
Punk'd and Skunked
The Blob That Ate Everyone
Into the Dark
Lights Out
No Survivors

Occupy Wall Street (or, *The Boy Who Ate Fear Street*)

The First Scream
It Came from the Internet
Help! We Have Strange Powers!
Bozos on Patrol
You Can't Scare Me!
Fight, Team, Fight!
Revenge of the Shadow People
The Loudest Scream
Do Some Damage!
Revenge R Us
Be Afraid—Be Very Afraid!

FRAGMENTS FROM *BAILOUT! THE MUSICAL*

Ben Greenman

Premiered: April 11, 2013
Performances: 119
Note: *Casting this musical proved challenging, as many of the characters in the opening scene are not human. Rather than use projections or animatronics, the producers decided to use small animals: dogs and cats were cast as Dollar Bill, Credit Card, and so forth, and their parts were sung by offstage actors. Ben Bernanke was played by Wallace Shawn.*

———

{A wallet is on a desk. A DOLLAR BILL pokes his head out.}

DOLLAR BILL

Let me introduce myself
I'm a dollar bill
Once I was the source
Of unlimited goodwill
People all around the world
Thought I was fantastic

The planet ran on paper
Before it ran on plastic
But now trust in me
Has been badly eroded
Thanks to lousy credit
I've been overloaded

{Next to him, a CREDIT CARD stirs.}

CREDIT CARD

I couldn't help but overhear
And I have to say I'm shocked
Why the hell would you blame me
And not blame common stocks?
Wasn't it the market
That fell down on the job
By appealing to the basest
Instincts of the mob?

{A STOCK CERTIFICATE rises off the desk nearby and unfolds.}

STOCK CERTIFICATE

Do you really think
That this bad feeling and rancor
Ever would have happened
If not for the bankers?
They're the ones who led us
Into rank overextension
The way that they have acted
Is beyond my comprehension

{The DOLLAR BILL, the CREDIT CARD, and the STOCK CERTIFI-CATE squabble. The DOLLAR BILL raises his voice. The STOCK CER-

*TIFICATE threatens the CREDIT CARD. Finally, a nearby CHECK-
BOOK speaks up.}*

CHECKBOOK

All of you, stop. Will you, please?
I don't want to see a fight
The truth is that you all are wrong
And also that you all are right
This fix we're in, you see
Is unimaginably complex
Monies are all intertwined
Y regresses onto X
Lehman, Merrill, AIG
No one knows a thing, you see
Let's all relax. Let's take a rest
The coolest heads can think the best
I have a film I want to show
Okay?

DOLLAR BILL

Okay.

CREDIT CARD

Okay.

STOCK CERTIFICATE

Let's go.

*{The CHECKBOOK pulls down a movie screen from the ceiling and, with
the CREDIT CARD's help, starts a projector. An image of Treasury Secretary HENRY PAULSON appears onscreen.}*

DOLLAR BILL

Who's the old guy?
He looks smart

CREDIT CARD

Shh . . . the movie's
About to start

{HENRY PAULSON speaks.}

HENRY PAULSON

Come now, travel with me
Back to 2001
Remember the big boom?
That was an awful lot of fun
Alan Greenspan warned
About the bursting bubble
He lowered all the interest rates
To try to forestall trouble
That led in turn to a big run
On purchases of real estate
Offset falling stock prices
With property? It all seemed great
But then the subprime borrowers
Started to default
And our proud economy
Began to grind to a halt

{The DOLLAR BILL snores.}

CREDIT CARD

What the hell?
The dollar's snoring

DOLLAR BILL

Sorry, guys
This movie's boring

{JOHN McCAIN appears onscreen.}

CHECKBOOK

It's going to get exciting quick
That guy with white hair is a maverick

{Onscreen, JOHN McCAIN speaks.}

JOHN McCAIN

I'm suspending my campaign
To focus on finance
This is a pressing, dire,
Unprecedented circumstance

My friends, I want to tell you
I'll work until the crisis ends
Nothing is more important
I hope you understand, my friends

The first debate must wait
The economy is failing
And sadly that will mean
Delaying Biden-Palin

{BARACK OBAMA objects to the postponement.}

BARACK OBAMA

What? You're kidding
You wouldn't dare
I'm going down to Mississippi

I'll expect to see you there

DOLLAR BILL

I don't get it at all
My friends? Mississippi?
This movie is weird
It's disjointed and trippy

{The CHECKBOOK stops the projector.}

STOCK CERTIFICATE

Come on, man. Don't stop the show
Dollar can't shut up, you know

CHECKBOOK

I won't restart the projector
It's off for the time being
I want to know that Dollar
Understands the things he's seeing

DOLLAR BILL

I understand—I'm sure I do
A financier once dropped a shoe
The second one was due for dropping
But in the meantime, he kept hopping

CHECKBOOK

I have to say that I'm not sure
I understand your metaphor

CREDIT CARD

This is insane

Let me explain

{*The CREDIT CARD turns to the DOLLAR BILL and speaks in a soft voice, trying not to lose his temper.*}

CREDIT CARD

Ben Bernanke
Met a bank he
Didn't like
Then another
And another
He called Mike
Bloomberg, and Bob Dole
Buffett, Nunn, and Volcker
Bernanke and Paulson then
Set up some very high-stakes poker
They bet that they could patch
The holes in the dike
With half a trillion dollars
And perhaps a small tax hike
They thought that now
Was the time to strike
Ben Bernanke
Met a bank he
Didn't like

DOLLAR BILL

Okay, Okay
Let's watch some more
I promise you
That I won't snore

{*The CHECKBOOK restarts the movie. In it, President GEORGE W. BUSH is presiding over an emergency meeting.*}

GEORGE W. BUSH

Let me start by saying
That I don't understand
A single thing about
The Invisible Hand
Or rates, or banks, or credit
Or mortgages or loans
But I know where my big desk is
And how to use the phones
And that is why I've called you
Here this afternoon
We need to fix this problem
And we need to fix it soon
A panic now is creeping
Over city, state, and town
If money isn't loosened up
This sucker could go down

{The group turns to WARREN BUFFETT for advice, since he is massively rich.}

WARREN BUFFETT

This economic Pearl Harbor
Has cooled off investors' ardor
Everything must be adjusted
We need some help or we'll be busted

{A $700 billion bailout is proposed. REPUBLICAN CONGRESSIO-NAL LEADERSHIP is displeased.}

REPUBLICAN CONGRESSIONAL LEADERSHIP

We remain staunchly defiant

Government can't get too giant
Seven hundred billion is an awful lot to spend
When we don't even know how deep the cracks extend

{The presidential candidates weigh in on the political implications of the crisis.}

JOHN McCAIN

Party lines are unimportant
We need a united front

BARACK OBAMA

So why'd you try to sink the debate?
It felt to some like a self-serving stunt

SARAH PALIN

Look! It's Russia, over there
Have I mentioned that I hunt?

{A compromise is reached. HENRY PAULSON and BEN BERNANKE announce it.}

HENRY PAULSON

Our commitment to financial health
Will soon restore the nation's wealth

BEN BERNANKE

It should recover fairly briskly
If not, you'll find me in the whiskey

{The film ends.}

DOLLAR BILL

Where's the rest?
I want to see how it turns out

CHECKBOOK

Well, it isn't over yet
We're in a time of fear and doubt
A major economic funk

DOLLAR BILL

I have to say, that movie stunk.

{The DOLLAR BILL, the CREDIT CARD, the STOCK CERTIFI-
CATE, and the CHECKBOOK decide to play cards instead. The DOLLAR
BILL, surprisingly, wins most of the hands.}

POLITICAL DECISION-MAKING IN THE NEW CENTURY

Sean Carman

President Obama and His Advisors on Inauguration Eve, 2009

CHIEF ADVISOR: Congratulations! Your landslide victory has given you a popular mandate to end the wars in Iraq and Afghanistan, close Guantánamo, pass universal health care, restore fairness to the tax code, strengthen environmental protection, and redistribute the concentration of wealth in America. Great job, Mr. President. You've done an amazing thing.

OBAMA: What should we do now?

CHIEF ADVISOR: Abandon all of it. Retreat to a moderate agenda of incremental management of the status quo.

OBAMA: Good idea. That is exactly what we will do.

Inside the Office of House Speaker John Boehner, 2011

ADVISOR: Mr. Speaker, if you could stop crying, even for one minute.

BOEHNER: (*crying*) The wolf bit Old Yeller. That's why they had to put him down.

ADVISOR: I know, sir. I know. But I was saying: the American people are frightened by the prolonged recession. They have no idea what's causing it, or how to fix it, but any bold plan that promises some economic improvement will win their support.

BOEHNER: (*drying his eyes*) It sounds like a political opportunity. What should we do?

ADVISOR: Terrorize the public into repealing Social Security with the threat of a government default on its loan obligations. In the process, we may accidentally bankrupt the country and wreck the global economy.

BOEHNER: (*still drying his eyes*) Whatever I pay you people, it is not enough. That is exactly what we will do.

Strategy Meeting in the Office of Sarah Palin, 2011

FIRST ADVISOR: We need to make a decision about whether you will run for president. The key primaries are coming up.

PALIN: Gosh darn it! The decisions just keep flying at me. But you know, you cannot blink. Remember that time when President McCain called me?

SECOND ADVISOR: The thing is, we have a lot of catching up to do.

PALIN: I remember being governor. Citizens came to me and said, "Sarah, how can we have prosperity?" For Alaskans, they meant. Because that's who we are, Alaskans. I think of those stars on our flag. You know they make the Big Dipper? Gold stars. A dipper is like a cup, but it's not a cup.

SECOND ADVISOR: If we could stay focused here—

PALIN: People feel they've lost something. Their country is no longer their own. We used to have a political system. But it's been taken away from us. And you know who did that?

FIRST ADVISOR: Ms. Palin, can you hear us?

PALIN: Not the oil companies, or other corporations. Because they are the job creators. I've seen this on the Slope. When Todd worked there, especially. Feeding those hungry markets.

SECOND ADVISOR: Hello! [*waving arms*] The presidency? Your decision to run? It's why we're here?

PALIN: It's the liberals and their radical ideas to eliminate job creation. And to not balance our budgets. Which are so important. They are to blame.

FIRST ADVISOR: I don't think it matters what we say.

PALIN: Because America has lost its way. That's the message. It's how people feel. And if that anger can be skillfully manipulated, by me, for example—

SECOND ADVISOR: She's in some sort of catatonic state, in which she's conscious and can speak. It's like she's channeling something.

FIRST ADVISOR: It's remarkable.

PALIN: Like when you're snowmobiling and you go off the path. But that path is America. It's our path.

FIRST ADVISOR: Maybe we should call a doctor.

SECOND ADVISOR: Yeah, good idea.

Strategy Meeting with New Jersey Governor Chris Christie, 2011

ADVISOR: Rick Perry is an ambulatory moron. Herman Cain's regressive tax proposals will never win a majority. Romney is basically a vacuum-cleaner salesman in a tailored suit. This is your moment. You can win this thing.

CHRISTIE: But no one knows anything about me. We'll be asking people to vote for someone they know almost nothing about.

ADVISOR: That is exactly why this will work.

Inside the Office of New York City Mayor Michael Bloomberg, 2011

ADVISOR: Brookfield Properties, one of the world's largest commercial real estate companies, and the owners of Zuccotti Park, say they want the protestors cleared out so they can clean the park.

BLOOMBERG: Wait. I thought it was called Liberty Plaza Park.

ADVISOR: It was. In 2006 Brookfield named the park after its U.S. chairman, John Zuccotti.

BLOOMBERG: They can do that?

ADVISOR: It's their park.

BLOOMBERG: How can a private company own a city park?

ADVISOR: United States Steel built the park in return for permission to construct its nearby headquarters in violation of local zoning ordinances. Later, they sold the park to Brookfield.

BLOOMBERG: Is the park dirty?

ADVISOR: Not really. Anyway, the protestors are cleaning it.

BLOOMBERG: So the park was a payoff to the city. And now its corporate owners want me to crush a public protest on the pretext that the park needs to be cleaned.

ADVISOR: That's basically it, yes.

BLOOMBERG: Sounds like I don't have a choice. Send in the police. But what are these kids protesting, anyway?

ADVISOR: Beats me, Your Honor. Something about corporate control of the political system. They don't have a written agenda.

BLOOMBERG: Well, then, how are we supposed to know what they're upset about?

ADVISOR: That's what everybody's asking, sir.

BLOOMBERG: If only we could uncover the roots of all these problems.

{Pause}

BLOOMBERG: Bah! Anyway, about my plans to win a fourth term: You said you had the donor spreadsheets?

Inside President Obama's First Reelection Strategy Session, 2011

ADVISOR: Well, our strategy of triangulation and compromise has driven your approval ratings to their lowest point. And it's election season. That means it's time to return to the populist rhetoric of ending the wars, closing Guantánamo, passing universal health care, restoring fairness to the tax code, strengthening environmental protection, and redistributing the concentration of wealth in America.

PRESIDENT OBAMA: Are you sure this is the right approach?

ADVISOR: It's either this or defend your record as a moderate incremental manager of the status quo.

PRESIDENT OBAMA: How often has that worked?

ADVISOR: Never, sir. It's never worked.

{Pause}

PRESIDENT OBAMA: I'm on board! When do we start?

FORMER CIA DIRECTOR GEORGE TENET'S OTHER EXCUSES

Christopher Monks

For Forgetting to Take Out the Garbage

You have to understand that I am a very busy man. Would I have liked to remember to take out the garbage? Yes. I'd be a fool not to want to have remembered to take out the garbage. It's just that I'm a very busy person with several different wastebaskets. I, of course, do take full responsibility for not emptying each one. However, my role as Household Director of Garbage is a lot more complicated than it may appear, and if people could walk in my shoes they would be surprised by the difficulty of my job. Thus, I doubt they'd be so eager to judge me about forgetting to take out the trash every once in a while.

For Accidentally Driving Over a Squirrel

It's common knowledge that when you're behind the wheel of an automobile you have numerous responsibilities: you're in charge of the speed of the vehicle, the temperature of the cabin, which radio station to listen to—the list goes on and on. So well before the squirrel jumped into the road, I, the driver, was held accountable for many different things. I should not have been, however, held accountable for the actions of a small, bushy, and, in this case, obviously suicidal rodent. Some say if I hadn't been changing the dial of the radio station when the squirrel bounded onto the road out of nowhere, this never would have happened. But how was I supposed to know what the squirrel was going to do? Besides, "Barracuda" by Heart was playing on the radio and that song annoys me to no end. Thus it was in the best interest and safety of all parties within the vehicle that I switch to a different channel. Otherwise I would have become very, very grumpy, and as those who are around me on a regular basis can attest, that does not make for a pleasant trip to Six Flags.

On Mistakenly Shoplifting a Carton of Eggs from the Automatic Checkout Lane at the Supermarket

We all know that the technology of the automatic checkout lane at the supermarket can be a little erratic at times. Sometimes an item scans; sometimes it does not. I was under the impression that the carton of eggs had scanned. However, in retrospect it appears it had not. Now, my critics suggest that I should return to Shop 'n Save and fess up to my indiscretion, but they don't understand the pressure I am under from my wife. She has a long, sordid history with Shop 'n Save, and believes that the free eggs are appropriate retribution for years of getting ripped off by their price gouging. So you see, it's really out of my hands. In a perfect world I'd return to pay for the eggs, but since I am not my household's Director of Grocery Shopping, there's really nothing I can do.

For Not Flossing Every Day

Look, I can only tell you my side of the conversation: I told my dental hygienist that I would do "my best" to floss every day. Now it's been reported that I had "promised" to floss every day, and that is absolutely false. I never promised my dental hygienist that I would floss every day. In my line of work you don't make promises you can't keep, so I exercise extreme restraint in using that word in my day-to-day dealings with people. Am I calling my dental hygienist a liar? No. I'm simply saying that she and I have differing opinions about how that conversation transpired. Do I wish I flossed every day? Yes. Of course I realize flossing is vital in the fight to keep my teeth and gums healthy, but you have to understand that I have many, many teeth and the job of keeping each one of them clean is a terribly complicated task. I have plenty to do and worry about as it is, what with the garbage and such, so the idea that I should be some superhero who takes complete care of his teeth is terribly unrealistic.

For Voting for Sanjaya on *American Idol*

Listen, we had a lot of intelligence about the program, and there were many people in my family who were convinced that Sanjaya Malakar was worthy of becoming the next American Idol. Now, there's this impression out there that we somehow "cooked the books" to convince ourselves that Sanjaya was the performer of mass distinction on the show. That is false. We simply used the information that we had gathered, which at the time we believed to be credible, and came to the conclusion that Sanjaya was the contestant to vote for. In the end, were we wrong? Clearly, his butchering of "Ain't No Mountain High Enough" proved that we were. But to say that we entered into this mission knowing we were going to vote for Sanjaya and steered our intelligence toward substantiating this goal is completely misguided.

A MESSAGE FROM A TSA FULL-BODY SCANNER

Jesse Adelman

There's been quite a bit of scuttlebutt in the press and amongst the civil-liberties crowd about what we—myself and my fellow full-body scanners—are coming to your airports to do. What is our real purpose? How invasive, truly, are these full-body scans? Will air travel, over time, become somehow less dignified, less "private"?

I'd like to take the opportunity of this writing to allay these and other misgivings. Please know: I'm just here to measure your penises. And I'm very, very good at it.

Can I see electronic components or liquid metals? Exotic bomb-making compounds? Timers or wires poking out of foreign orifices that mean us harm? No, no, and no, I cannot. And ladies, I have no interest in whatever arrangements you might have going on down there—no thanks! Fundamentally, I'm a specialist. I was built to measure penises for national security.

Many folks seem to have the impression that their penis scans will simply be appraised by a crew of chuckling, fantastically overweight elementary-school dropouts in some musty back room near the baggage drop. While that may well be the case, you can rest assured that your penis will be regarded with the utmost professional care and clinical detachment until the very moment that a fine-grained digital image of your business leaves my fiber-optic cable en route to our vast federal crotch database.

I'm not just some dumb consumer SKU scanner from Epson, repurposed and jammed inside a futuristic beige plastic enclosure and stamped with a TSA logo. I've scanned the novels of Proust, Flaubert, and Turgenev, in addition to literally hundreds of thousands of pages of pornographic magazines. I can tell the difference between your penis and a breakfast sausage, a sock monkey, and a cat's bladder stuffed with warm oatmeal. I am an expert. I am ready to serve.

For nearly a decade, lightly trained TSA employees have been forced to estimate—to guess, really—your penis size, based on such factors as height, weight, walking style, and disposition. Frankly, that's asking them to do the impossible. It gratifies me to think that millions of travelers will now be able to fly just a little bit easier, secure in the knowledge of their newly complete and accurate TSA profiles—all thanks to my precise genital scans. I can verify your length, girth, heft, and other major identifying characteristics. Everything but the color; this is America, and we don't do that here.

In some quarters, folks have been asking, "Why?" As in, "Why must the Department of Homeland Security build and maintain a vast database comprising digital images and noteworthy attributes of the penises of domestic and international travelers?" Questions like these are not for me to answer; I'm just a full-body scanner, not a political appointee. And if this issue is above my pay grade, surely it's above yours—after all, you don't even work for the Transportation Security Administration.

The salient point is this: Uncle Sam needs to know exactly what you're packing for the War on Terror. As long as you've got something halfway reasonable down the front of those sweatpants, what do any of us really have to worry about?

A GUEST COLUMNIST STILL GETTING THE HANG OF IT

Ellie Kemper

Four hundred thousand deaths every year—and growing. From smoking, I mean. Deaths from smoking. Nearly half a million people are dying from smoking-related things every year. Americans, that is. I'm talking about half a million Americans. I don't have the numbers of smoking-related deaths in other countries. But four hundred thousand Americans dying from smoking every year: that's bad. And I am not exactly sure what we should do about it.

Global warming is the biggest threat facing the globe today. Second-biggest threat. Terrorism, then global warming. Or maybe the reverse. At any rate, I will mention that teen pregnancy is also on the rise. Some people consider that a threat. Me, I'm not so sure that's a threat. My mother had me when she was nineteen, and on purpose. So that was not such a bad thing. Make love, not war, right? To an extent.

The point is that the globe is heating up, terrorists are trying to rule the world, and babies keep popping out of teenaged girls. All of these things should be addressed. At some point, we will also need to figure out what to do about DVD pirating.

Christina Williams is a typical high-school freshman on the outskirts of Pittsburgh. She is captain of the cheerleading squad, an active member of the French Club, and just beginning to learn tae kwon do. Christina has a steady boyfriend who loves her, for the most part, and a weekend job serving ice cream at the local Scoops. She hopes to go into law or real estate when she grows up, and recently organized a highly successful bake sale to raise awareness of France.

Christina Williams doesn't have health insurance.

As for Afghanistan, I must say I'm a little torn on this issue. I can sort of see all sides of the argument. Do we increase troops or withdraw? Do we keep the deadline or play it by ear? I don't really have an answer. If we increase troops, then that equals more Americans fighting what some might consider a hopeless war. If we completely withdraw now, then we will leave an extraordinary mess behind us. Setting a deadline seems pretty pointless. But if we play it by ear, then we might not feel any sense of urgency. The whole thing is nothing short of a complete disaster. Yikes!!

When exactly did the Catholic Church become such an enormous institution? Don't get me wrong. I admire religion, but this particular one seems a tad too organized—and large. That being said, I will admit that I sort of like this current Pope. Having said that, I should mention that I don't like him very much. He tends to say some pretty outrageous things. Though I do admire his chutzpah.

Dolphins keep getting snared in nets meant for tuna, but I wouldn't exactly advise a ban on tuna. There is no point in throwing out the baby with the bathwater—although maybe there is. However, a tuna ban seems pretty implausible. A lot of people really enjoy tuna fish.

What is the deal with these immigrants?

I would love to hear my readers' feedback. Most of what I write depends on what inspires me. And you, the readership, inspire me. So please send any comments, thoughts, questions, or concerns my way. I look forward to reading them.

Please send only positive feedback. I get anxious.

EXTENDED TRAILER FOR *AMERICAN DEMOGRAPHIC 2012*

Pete Reynolds

{*Scene opens at a county fair in Middle America. PRESIDENT OBAMA is seated in a dunk tank, with the target to his right and the water below. DAVID AXELROD stands next to the tank, looking concerned.*}

AXELROD: Mr. President, as your chief political strategist, I have to advise against this.

PRESIDENT OBAMA: David, as you know, I am up for reelection. I need to reconnect with the voters in a way that allows for a civil exchange of ideas and concerns.

AXELROD: I'm just not sure this format—

PRESIDENT OBAMA:—Shhh! Here comes a future Obama supporter now.

{*DISSATISFIED LIBERAL approaches the dunk tank and picks up a baseball.*}

DISSATISFIED LIBERAL: Hello, I am Dissatisfied Liberal. I expected you to both change the hyperpartisan culture of Washington and implement an unabashedly progressive agenda. In no way are those two notions incompatible.

PRESIDENT OBAMA: I hear your concerns. There are entrenched interests and partisan gamesmanship on both sides of the aisle, and—

{DISSATISFIED LIBERAL uncorks a pitch, but it sails wide left.}

PRESIDENT OBAMA: Hey, what the hell, man?

DISSATISFIED LIBERAL: I will now betray your location to my fellow travelers, Disillusioned Young Person and Disappointed Hollywood Celebrity. I am pretending that I won't vote for you, but I almost certainly will.

{As DISSATISFIED LIBERAL walks off toward the Tilt-A-Whirl, PRESIDENT OBAMA notices WALMART MOM sitting at a nearby picnic table, clipping coupons.}

PRESIDENT OBAMA: Ma'am, I am President Obama, and I share your concerns about the state of the economy. Please join me at the dunk tank.

WALMART MOM: Oh, good. I was wondering what to do with all these baseballs the bald guy with the glasses gave me.

{As WALMART MOM walks over, PRESIDENT OBAMA scans the concession-stand area and sees KARL ROVE handing out grocery sacks full of baseballs to passersby.}

WALMART MOM: Hello, Mr. President. I am Walmart Mom. I am concerned about rising unemployment and the high cost of consumer goods. I am apparently shorthand for anyone who is not extremely wealthy and has borne children.

PRESIDENT OBAMA: My policies aim to create jobs for people just like you.

WALMART MOM: And don't forget about my husband, Working-Class White. We used to be Soccer Mom and NASCAR Dad, but that was back when we could afford to care about recreation. Now we fret about financial ruin.

{WALMART MOM returns to her coupons at the picnic table. As PRESIDENT OBAMA and AXELROD watch her go, KARL ROVE tiptoes up to the side of the dunk tank and starts slipping in live jellyfish.}

PRESIDENT OBAMA: Karl, how's it going? Cool jellyfish.

AXELROD: Karl, no! NO. You hear me? Now get on out of here! Go on! Get!

{AXELROD shoos away KARL ROVE, who scampers off, clicking his heels and cackling wildly. While PRESIDENT OBAMA leans over to take a look at the jellyfish, he notices a message scrawled onto the wall of the tank in blue ink: "G. W. Bush was hear." Suddenly, the echo of KARL ROVE's laughter is replaced by the sound of an approaching snare drum, signaling the arrival of TEA PARTIER, dressed for the occasion in colonial-era garb.}

AXELROD: Welcome to the fair. I assume you'd like a baseball?

TEA PARTIER: Thank you, sir, but no. I am Tea Partier, and I am very fond of symbolism. I would prefer to knock this "president" off his perch and into the dunk tank using only this bound edition of *The Federalist Papers* and this laminated copy of the U.S. Constitution.

{TEA PARTIER grunts as he throws a hotel Bible and a Waffle House menu at the target. He does not connect.}

TEA PARTIER: Traitor!

{TEA PARTIER resumes his march through the fair.}

PRESIDENT OBAMA: Hey, I like your wig!

{As TEA PARTIER walks away, we see that a "Kick Me" sign has been taped to his back. Just then, a snickering VICE PRESIDENT BIDEN sneaks out from behind the Funhouse and immediately starts chucking an armload of baseballs at the target.}

PRESIDENT OBAMA: Joe, hey! Joe! What are you doing, buddy?!

BIDEN: Oh, hey, Barack! Some guy over there's just giving these things away!

{He unleashes one more, which just misses the target.}

BIDEN: Hey, who's up for a brew? David Whacks-his-rod?

AXELROD: *{stares blankly at Biden}*

{BIDEN plays an air-guitar riff and skips off in the direction of the "Guess Your Weight" barker, just as a black stretch limousine pulls up. Mounted on the rear of the car is an enormous, mechanized catapult full of baseballs. The DRIVER, who looks suspiciously like TIMOTHY GEITHNER, hops out to open the back passenger-side door. A well-dressed gentleman—WALL STREET BANKER—steps out.}

WALL STREET BANKER: Hello, I am Wall Street Banker. My shoes are made of platinum and mink heart, and my pants are lined with warm ocean breezes and the souls of saints.

AXELROD: Hello, Wall Street Banker. Please, make yourself comfortable. Can we get you anything from the concession stand? A corndog, perhaps? Twinkie milkshake? Fried chocolate cheeseburger-pancake?

WALL STREET BANKER: I just made an infinite amount of money in the time it took you to list those proletarian delicacies.

PRESIDENT OBAMA: Bacon maple chili-cheese funnel cake?

WALL STREET BANKER: I just invented a new type of security made entirely of poor people's childhood memories.

AXELROD: Donut-glaze-Thousand-Island-mozzarella-stick sundae?

WALL STREET BANKER: I just sold four hundred million dollars' worth of my new securities.

PRESIDENT OBAMA: A Mason jar full of shortening?

WALL STREET BANKER: And I just earned five hundred million by destroying the value of my new securities. Driver!

DRIVER: Sir?

WALL STREET BANKER: My private chopper is just beyond that crowd of children playing with shelter puppies. Get there as fast as possible.

DRIVER: Yes, sir.

WALL STREET BANKER: Driver!

DRIVER: Sir?

WALL STREET BANKER: While you're at it, go ahead and cut the brake line.

DRIVER: Yes, sir.

WALL STREET BANKER: You know what they say: time is money, but puppy carcasses are decidedly not money.

{WALL STREET BANKER and the DRIVER climb back in the car. After a brief hesitation, the limo-pult peels out. PRESIDENT OBAMA and AXELROD cough and wave away the cloud of dust hovering over the dunk tank.}

AXELROD: Mr. President, you have a schedule to keep. We should be going. Besides, I just received word that an anonymous right-wing billionaire hired Justin Verlander, Félix Hernández, and C. C. Sabathia, and he's flying them to this very dunk tank as we speak.

PRESIDENT OBAMA: All right, let's go. I think this went well.

AXELROD: I'm glad, Mr. President.

PRESIDENT OBAMA: Uh . . . David?

AXELROD: Yes, Mr. President?

PRESIDENT OBAMA: How do I get out of this thing?

AXELROD: That's a great question.

YOUR ATTEMPTS TO LEGISLATE AGAINST HUNTING MAN FOR SPORT REEK OF CLASS WARFARE

Mike Lacher

Our nation is being rent asunder. Some Americans are content to watch their freedoms slip away as politicians turn one citizen against another, but I will not be one of them. Today, I draw my line in the sand. I refuse, with every ounce of my God-given American blood, to allow my right to hunt man for sport to be used in a pathetic partisan ploy to engage our country in class warfare.

Liberty can be heard from many places in this great nation of ours: in the voices of children reciting the Pledge of Allegiance, in the crack of a baseball bat on opening day, or in the quiet thud of a well-paid drifter falling lifeless upon a riverbank after being tagged by a scoped rifle fired from the highest hill of a private game reserve. My remote compound in the middle of the Everglades is the one place where I can relax and enjoy the fruits of my labors, where I can turn off my cell phone, turn on my night-vision goggles, and worry about nothing but whether the rustle in the drapes is just the wind or a crafty target who managed to incapacitate my guards without tripping the lasers on the portico.

Now, as always happens in an economic downturn, the liberal politicians have begun making pariahs out of those who only want to hunt the most dangerous game in peace. They engage in their petty populism, trying to turn those who do not hunt man against those who do. But do they not think every American wishes they had the means to take first blood of a man on the field of sport and cunning? Do they not think my oak-paneled wall of mounted index fingers serves as a manifestation of the American dream for so many factory workers and cubicle dwellers? Perhaps they think that when a middle-class laborer rests his head on his pillow he does not see gleaming visions of stalking through the reeds with nothing but his wits, a machete, and a pith helmet.

I apologize, Mr. Senator, for working hard enough in foreign munitions brokering to have established the means to hunt the occasional human from sundown Thursday until sunrise Monday. I apologize for being so bold as to provide valuable economic activity by spending thousands of dollars on platinum-tipped cartridges, GPS-triggered explosive collars, and platter upon platter of charcuterie. And I apologize, ever so deeply, for having the unmitigated temerity to cruise the back alleys of Miami and offer hopeless drifters the chance to make a fortune in a few days, or at least end their pathetic lives while knowing what it feels like to be a jungle king.

Prohibit my passion, destroy my dreams, shutter the gates on my compound, and throw out my fleet of manservants, many of whom are too undereducated and scarred by birdshot to ever work in retail or a similar field. Earn yourself a few votes come November and sit happily behind your desks for a few more years. But when the sad remains of what you have left of America turn back the pages of history, will you be such heroes, such crusaders for good? I tell you no, for when the people of America look at their faded nation wrapped in the tatters of empire, its red stripes bleached by cowardice, they will see the seizing of my rifles and the bulldozing of my booby-trapped portico as the tragic bellwethers of the end of an era.

LITTLE HOUSING CRISIS ON THE PRAIRIE

Susan Schorn

Laura and Mary got up early the next morning, for Pa was arranging the financing that day. They rode across the prairie in the covered wagon for a long time. Finally, they stopped.

"Here is where our house will be!" Pa said. Laura and Mary hurried to look. All around them stretched the prairie. For miles and miles, there was only grass and prairie hens and wild creatures.

"Where is the school?" Ma asked.

"Where is the golf course?" Mary wondered.

"Where will the tax base come from to support the development of adequate infrastructure?" Laura wanted to know.

"Now, Laura, don't pester," Ma said.

But Pa chuckled. "Well, little half-pint," he told Laura, "all those things are right here, just waiting to be built with good old American know-how, elbow grease, and stick-to-itiveness."

"And perseverance," Ma added.

"That, too," Pa agreed.

Just then Jack, the brindle bulldog, barked. A man Laura and Mary had never seen before rode up on a mule.

"Hullo, Edwards," Pa sang out. "Caroline, this is our neighbor, Mr. Edwards. I met him yesterday down at the creek. Mr. Edwards is a wildcat mortgage broker from Tennessee. He is going to finance our house for us."

"I am pleased to meet you, ma'am," Mr. Edwards said, bowing. "And I'm tickled to be able to offer you and your husband the finest 5/1 negative-amortization loan this side of the Mississippi."

"Tell us more," Pa encouraged him.

"Well, now, your teaser rate is only one point five percent," Mr. Edwards went on, pausing to spit tobacco juice. "Don't that beat all?"

"It sounds wonderful," Ma said politely in her gentle voice. "And what will our rate be after the introductory period, Mr. Edwards?"

"That depends on those scoundrels in Washington!" Mr. Edwards declared hotly.

"Pa, how much will we pay for the house?" Mary asked.

"What we pay doesn't matter much, Mary," Pa explained. "At one point five percent interest, we can easily service the debt on the principal."

Laura was confused. "But when do we pay off the principal, Pa?" she asked.

"She's got you there, Edwards," Pa laughed. "What about that principal?"

"Those are two mighty smart daughters you have there, Ingalls," Mr. Edwards said admiringly. "Well, it's pretty simple. Your loan will re-amortize every sixty months. The minimum payment will be recalculated at that time, but your rate will vary annually according to the then-current prime lending rate. Of course, your regular rate and payment resets will continue to apply, but these will be capped at—Look! A jackrabbit!"

"Good game surely is plentiful in this country," Pa observed.

"You've said it, Ingalls," Mr. Edwards agreed. "And once all the Indians are gone this land will be worth millions."

"That's true enough, Edwards," said Pa. "But you are taking the short view. I'm minded to give mortgages to all the Indians and sell them more houses."

Mr. Edwards whooped and threw his coonskin cap high in the

air. "Now, that's the kind of thinking that made this country great!" he shouted. "Why, we can issue mortgage-backed securities with a weighted average gross coupon of nine or ten percent!"

"We'll live like kings!" Pa exclaimed.

"Ingalls, you're the brokerin'est fool that ever I did see," Mr. Edwards told him, spitting into his mule's ear.

Pa and Ma signed the papers.

Laura still didn't understand. "But, Pa," she asked again, "if we never pay off any of the principal, how will we build equity in the house?"

"Don't worry, Laura," Pa reassured her. "In a year, this house will be worth twice what we paid for it. And if we need cash before then, I can always hew some equity out of an oak stump with my ax. Oak is good hard wood."

Then Laura felt better. Pa could make anything with his ax.

"You see, Laura," Pa went on, "Uncle Sam has made a bet with us. We have bet that housing prices will continue to rise at historic rates for the foreseeable future. And the government has bet that if real estate values plummet, honest citizens like us will be too stupid to do anything but continue paying out our hard-earned five-cent pieces for property that was never worth more than a fraction of its appraised value. Either way, we are going to win that bet!"

"Charles," Ma remonstrated. She did not approve of gambling, even in metaphors.

"But what if land values *do* drop?" Laura wanted to know.

Pa's blue eyes twinkled. "That can never happen, half-pint. Why, it's just as likely that all our crops will be ruined by a blizzard, or a prairie fire, or a horde of grasshoppers."

Laura and Mary and Ma and Pa all laughed at that idea. Jack barked and barked. Mr. Edwards ran around his mule in circles, slapping at imaginary bees.

"And I'll tell you what else, Caroline," Pa added. "As soon as the house is built and the oats are planted, I will drive the wagon to Independence and bring back some granite countertops for your kitchen."

Laura and Mary hugged each other at the thought of a house with boughten countertops.

"Oh, Charles!" Ma protested. "Store-boughten countertops! But Independence is forty miles away!"

"Pshaw, nothing's too good for you, Caroline," Pa told her. "Besides, I can put it on the credit card."

"Well," Ma admitted, "it will be nice to live like civilized folks again."

ATLAS SHRUGGED UPDATED FOR THE FINANCIAL CRISIS

Jeremiah Tucker

1.

"Damn it, Dagny! I need the government to get out of the way and let me do my job!"

She sat across the desk from him. She appeared casual but confident, a slim body with rounded shoulders like an exquisitely engineered truss. How he hated his debased need for her, he who loathed self-sacrifice but would give up everything he valued to get in her pants . . . Did she know?

"I heard the thugs in Washington were trying to take your Rearden Metal at the point of a gun," she said. "Don't let them, Hank. With your advanced alloy and my high-tech railroad, we'll revitalize our country's failing infrastructure and make big, virtuous profits."

"Oh, no, I got out of that sucker's game. I now run my own hedge fund firm, Rearden Capital Management."

"What?"

He stood and adjusted his suit jacket so that his body didn't betray his shameful weakness. He walked toward her and sat informally on the edge of her desk. "Why make a product when you can make dollars? Right this second, I'm earning millions in interest off money I don't even have."

He gestured to his floor-to-ceiling windows, a symbol of his productive ability and goodness.

"There's a whole world out there of byzantine financial products just waiting to be invented, Dagny. Let the leeches run my factories into the ground! I hope they do! I've taken out more insurance on a single Rearden Steel bond than the entire company is even worth! When my old company finally tanks, I'll make a cool eight hundred and seventy-seven million."

Their eyes locked with an intensity she was only beginning to understand. Yes, Hank . . . claim me . . . If we're to win the battle against the leeches, we must get it on . . . right now . . . Don't let them torture us for our happiness . . . or our billions.

He tore his eyes away.

"I can't. Sex is base and vile!"

"No, it's an expression of our highest values and our admiration for each other's minds."

"Your mind gives me the biggest boner, Dagny Taggart."

He fell upon her like a savage, wielding his mouth like a machete, and in the pleasure she took from him her body became an extension of her quarterly earnings report—proof of her worthiness as a lover. His hard-on was sanction enough.

"Scream your secret passions, Hank Rearden!"

"Derivatives!"

"Yes!"

"Credit-default swaps!"

"Oh, yes! Yes!"

"Collateralized debt obligations!"

"YES! YES! YES!"

2.

Dagny and Hank searched through the ruins of the Twenty-First Century Investment Bank. As they stepped through the crumbling cubicles, a trampled legal pad with a complex column of computations captured Dagny's attention. She fell to her hands and knees and raced through the pages and pages of complex math written in a steady hand. Her fingers bled from the paper cuts, and she did not care.

"What is it, Dagny?"

"Read this."

"Good God!"

"Yes, it's an experimental formula for a financial strategy that could convert static securities into kinetic profits that would increase at an almost exponential rate."

Hank studied the numbers. "The amount of debt you would need to make this work would be at least thirty to one, but a daring, rational man who lives by his mind would be willing to take that risk!"

"Yes, and it's so complex the government could never regulate it."

"It's perfect. There's only one problem—half the pages are missing. Could you reconstruct it, Dagny?"

Her answer escaped her lips like air from a punctured galvanized-steel duct: "No."

"I didn't think so, but why leave such an achievement to rot here? It's the greatest thing I've ever laid eyes on, made by a monumental genius, the sort of mind that's only born once in a century . . . Dagny, why are you fondling your breasts?"

3.

There was still the breathless tone in her voice when she asked, "The financial strategy . . . the financial strategy I found . . . it was you who made it?"

"Yes," he said.

John Galt's face betrayed no signs of pain or fear or guilt, and his body had the clean tensile strength of a foundry casting, with skin the color of a polished full-port brass valve. In the center of this secret mountain valley where the titans of Wall Street had retreated for an extended junket was a three-foot-tall dollar sign of pure gold atop a granite column. It was tacky, yes, but it was also their emblem, a symbol of their triumph.

"But why did you leave it behind?"

"Because once I committed the plan to memory I no longer needed it."

"I don't understand."

"The capital-gains tax, Dagny," Galt said. "We loathe it."

He pointed to the houses of men she knew, and the names sounded like the richest stock market in the world—a roll call of honor.

"Our money represents our spirit's values," Galt said. "When the government takes our profits, it is literally robbing us of our souls. I will not apologize for my wealth to a nation of looters. We who live by the mind could've been engineers, scientists, doctors, extreme-sports enthusiasts, but there is no purer pursuit than the pursuit of money. A is A. Money begets more money, and . . . "

Galt went on like this for what seemed to Dagny like hours, until, finally, something he said piqued her interest.

"And that's why I created the financial plan you found. It's true, it works. But it is not sustainable. It will ruin this country's financial system, and then we'll see how those who despise us prosper when their lenders and investors refuse to invest or lend." He laughed joylessly. "Funny, isn't it? I must destroy the very thing I love in order to save it."

"Just to avoid paying taxes?"

"I do not compromise my beliefs, and I will kill anyone who asks me to!"

A silence fell between them, and it was awkward.

Finally, Dagny asked, "So, just out of curiosity, how much are you worth?"

He shrugged. "What is infinity?"

She let out a rich, powerful moan, like the sound of a passing diesel train in the night.

NOISES THAT SELECT POLITICAL PUNDITS WOULD MAKE IF THEY WERE WILD ANIMALS INSTEAD OF POLITICAL PUNDITS

John Warner

Chuck Todd: blagoo-ORGH blagoo-ORGH blagoo-ORGH thfffffft

Ann Coulter: SNEEEEEEEERRRRRGOOOOOPlah fleck fleck

Peggy Noonan: blah blah blah blah hummmm I WORKED FOR REAGAN hummmmmm blahhhhhh

William Kristol: PAMP-poo NOR Pamp-poo nog NOR PAMP-poo NOR Pamp-poo nog NOR PAMP-poo NOR Pamp-poo nog NOR PAMP-poo NOR Pamp-poo nog NOR morgh morgh morgh PAMP-poo NOR Pamp-poo nog NOR PAMP-poo NOR Pamp-poo nog NOR PAMP-poo NOR Pamp-poo nog NOR morgh morgh morgh PAMP-poo NOR Pamp-poo nog NOR PAMP-poo NOR Pamp-poo nog NOR morgh

Juan Williams: cheep cheep cheep cheep cheep cheep cheep cheep

George F. Will: blurg

DONALD RUMSFELD: LOVE DOCTOR

Stephen Elliott

In love there are things you know, and things you don't know, and things you don't know you don't know.

You can't share your feelings with your lover when you don't know what those feelings are.

Arguments of convenience lack integrity and inevitably trip you up.

Don't treat your lover in a way you wouldn't want to see on the front page of the *Washington Post*.

Don't speak ill of your girlfriend's ex-boyfriends. Enjoy your time together; it may well be one of the most interesting and challenging times of your life.

First rule of love: you can't win unless you're on the ballot.

I don't do quagmires.

If you screw up, talk it out; delays only compound mistakes.

In our system relationships require consent, not command.

Every day in every relationship is filled with numerous opportunities for serious error; enjoy it.

It is easier to get into something than to get out of it. It isn't making mistakes that's critical, it's correcting them.

Leave your lover's family business to them; you'll have plenty to do without trying to manage the First Family.

Let your friends know you're still the same person. Look for what's missing; your friends can tell you how to improve, but they can't help you see what isn't there.

Preserve your lover's options; she needs them.

The price of being close to another human being is delivering bad news; you fail them when you don't tell the truth.

The way to do well is to do well.

If possible, visit the ex; they know the ropes and can help you see around corners.

When raising an issue with your lover, try to come away with a decision; pose issues so as to evoke guidance.

You will launch many projects but have time to finish only a few.

Your new girlfriend is not your old girlfriend.

Your performance in a relationship depends on your significant other; select the best.

Death has a tendency to encourage a depressing view of war.

PARALLELS BETWEEN MY LIVING THROUGH TWO YEARS OF MIDDLE SCHOOL AND THE TWO TERMS OF GEORGE W. BUSH'S PRESIDENCY

Teddy Wayne

The radical changes going on around me make me uncomfortable.

I am unhappy about the way things are, but feel helpless to do anything about it.

Shame is my dominant emotion.

I feel very insecure and vulnerable.

Others supposedly feel as I do, but whenever I turn on the TV it seems otherwise.

At times, I wish I lived in a faraway country.

I want to rebel against anyone in a position of authority.

Social mobility is a fallacy.

I find myself frequently watching sports for comfort.

It's totally unfair that when I screw up I get in trouble, but when my superiors do, nothing happens.

What I represent is repugnant to foreign women.

Flying is much more terrifying than it should be.

When I talk to friends on the phone, I'm afraid someone is listening in.

People tell me things will only improve after this, but I don't believe it.

I constantly think the world is going to end.

I really dislike the arrogant popular guy elected as my president.

French is considered lame.

REPUBLICAN S&M SAFE WORDS

Nathan Pensky

Trickle Down
Surge
Cut and Run
Bait and Switch
Flip-Flop
Wide Stance
Gerrymander

FRAGMENTS FROM *WEINER! THE MUSICAL*

Ben Greenman

Premiered: January 9, 2013
Performances: 912
Note: *This musical exceeded all expectations, setting box-office records for topical musicals and charming most of the critics. One influential critic, Martin Rebosco of the* Daily Dose, *was not as impressed. "This morning," he wrote, "I had an upset stomach, and at breakfast it began to rumble something terrible. Before I could reach the toilet or the sink or even the trash can, I disgorged a terribly large quantity of something liquid and yellowish. This musical is the equivalent. Turn off the dork, if you know what I mean." Despite Rebosco's resistance, the musical served as the launching pad for a number of movie stars, including Henry Chester, who debuted in the title role and has gone on to star in several hit films, including the James Bond reboot* Excitement 3000!

———

{*ANTHONY WEINER sits at home, bored.*}

ANTHONY WEINER

I was an early bloomer

I started with Chuck Schumer
As his protégé
That's my résumé.

{ANTHONY WEINER goes to the window, still bored, and sings.}

ANTHONY WEINER

So many nights I feel nervous
This life I've led of public service
Has left me feeling dull and out of sorts
I've read some books. I've watched some sports
But evening drags. The sun's long set
Should I just go to sleep? Not yet.

{ANTHONY WEINER, pacing his apartment, spies a computer. Evidently he has not seen one before.}

ANTHONY WEINER

What is this box with wires and screen,
This intoxicating machine?
I will sit down and touch a key
Oh listen, how it speaks to me.

{ANTHONY WEINER begins to use the computer. Soon he can do nothing else.}

ANTHONY WEINER

I once watched sports and also read
But in those days my brain was dead
Now it's alive and so am I
Across the wired world I fly
I click, I blog, I surf, I Tweet
My life, once partial, is now complete.

{ANTHONY WEINER begins to meet women online.}

ANTHONY WEINER

In our many cybermeetings
We have had great conversations
There is something intimate
About these wired communications.

FEMALE SCREEN NAME #1

I agree completely,
Total stranger.
We can talk without
A hint of danger.

ANTHONY WEINER

I have a wife
In real life
But somehow I feel closer still
To distant places
And unseen faces
You inspire in me a deep goodwill.

FEMALE SCREEN NAME #2

Me, too. I know just what you mean.
You can tell me anything onscreen.

{ANTHONY WEINER's wife, HUMA ABEDIN, grows briefly suspicious.}

HUMA ABEDIN

Hey, what's going on in here?
I hope nothing degrading.

ANTHONY WEINER

Don't be suspicious, dear
Only some day-trading.

{The online conversations begin to turn flirtatious.}

ANTHONY WEINER

The way you make me feel, you know
Is making my trust grow and grow.

FEMALE SCREEN NAME #3

I hope you don't just mean your trust
I rubbed the keyboard on my bust.

ANTHONY WEINER

Can I call you on the phone?
Can we have a kind of date?

FEMALE SCREEN NAME #4

The prospect of your voice, you know
Makes my pulse accelerate.

ANTHONY WEINER

I took my shoes off, and my shirt.

FEMALE SCREEN NAME #5

The thought of that just drenched my skirt.

{ANTHONY WEINER, taken by the charms of FEMALE SCREEN NAMES #1–#5, considers sending explicit photographs.}

ANTHONY WEINER

I have been struggling as of late
Deciding if it's right or wrong
To use these social-network sites
To send a picture of your schlong.

{His TINY CONSCIENCE speaks up.}

ANTHONY WEINER'S TINY CONSCIENCE

What the hell?
Are you kidding, man?
That's your question?
That's your plan?

ANTHONY WEINER

Well, not even the schlong exposed!
But inside boxer briefs and posed
To look much larger than it is
So, gasping, they'll say, "Is that his?"

ANTHONY WEINER'S TINY CONSCIENCE

Holy crap,
You're serious?
I feel such a
Weariness.

ANTHONY WEINER

Look, I've thought the matter through
And this is what I'll say to you:
I'm a firebrand in the Congress
I know the right wing's dirty tricks
I work with great determination

To kick against the pricks
So it's noteworthy that I can't think
Of a reason not to Tweet my dink.

ANTHONY WEINER'S TINY CONSCIENCE

I don't know quite how to respond.
My only recourse is to shrink.

{ANTHONY WEINER'S TINY CONSCIENCE leaves. ANTHONY WEINER takes a picture of himself, erect, in underwear. He intends to send it privately but accidentally posts it online. The image is captured by bloggers, and ANTHONY WEINER is asked about it.}

ANTHONY WEINER

I sent nothing
Stop this chatter
This isn't an
Important matter
I'm a rising legislative star
How stupid do you think I are?

{After refusing to flatly deny that he is the man pictured, ANTHONY WEINER calls a press conference during which he admits his guilt.}

ANTHONY WEINER

What I did was wrong, if not quite a crime.
I didn't think things through at all
My behavior truly was horrendous
My arrogance and nerve stupendous
But I won't resign at the present time
I will let that be the voters' call.

{REPORTERS begin to ask questions.}

REPORTER #1

Will you be shutting down your Twitter?

REPORTER #2

Are you sure the women were of age?

REPORTER #3

Why isn't your wife by your side?

REPORTER #4

Why'd you let Breitbart take the stage?

REPORTER #5

Do you think the photo of your chest
Really shows off your body best?

{ANTHONY WEINER answers the questions patiently, sometimes showing emotion. On his way out, he is cornered by a gang. As they emerge from the shadows, he sees that they are MARK SANFORD, ARNOLD SCHWARZENEGGER, ELIOT SPITZER, JIM McGREEVEY, and LARRY CRAIG.}

MARK SANFORD

For years and years I ruled over
The great state of South Carolina
But then I lost my kingdom for
A South American vagina.

ARNOLD SCHWARZENEGGER

When the maid came in
To clean the room

I said, "I'll be back—
Inside your womb."

ELIOT SPITZER

In the days I was Client Nine
I had a massive credit line
A call girl is a man's best friend
Except, of course, for CNN.

JIM McGREEVEY

I tried to change the state song
To "Macho Man" or "In the Navy"
I served the public well and also
Served up some McGreevey Gravy.

ANTHONY WEINER

You are all quite well-known cases
Of elected, then dishonored, males
Have you come before me now as
Chastened cautionary tales?

{The others look around, confused.}

ELIOT SPITZER

No—the reason we've materialized
Is to tell you that we're all surprised.

JIM McGREEVEY

Surprised and also disappointed
Our secret brotherhood anointed
You to be our true successor
But your offense is sadly lesser.

{JIM McGREEVEY moves to hit ANTHONY WEINER. ARNOLD SCHWARZENEGGER stops him.}

ARNOLD SCHWARZENEGGER

Wait. How many kids did you put in her?

ANTHONY WEINER

We didn't have sex.

ARNOLD SCHWARZENEGGER

What? Are you sure?
Why would you risk career and home
Without spraying your baby foam?

{ARNOLD SCHWARZENEGGER shoves ANTHONY WEINER, after which LARRY CRAIG delivers a series of kicks.}

LARRY CRAIG

I lost it all in a bathroom stall
My life went down the toilet quick
A picture of your underwear?
You amateur: you make me sick
Stop squirming, Weiner. Just stay put.
That pain you feel is my tapping foot.

{ANTHONY WEINER closes his eyes and lets himself be beaten. Suddenly, the violence stops. He opens his eyes. The men are gone. He stands and looks around. He sees only his TINY CONSCIENCE.}

ANTHONY WEINER

Hi there, conscience. Welcome back.
Thanks for stopping the attack.

That Larry Craig has a short fuse.

ANTHONY WEINER'S TINY CONSCIENCE

I'm sad to say I have bad news.
While you were taking pictures in your tightie-whities
I went up to heaven and spoke to the Almighty.

{THE ALMIGHTY steps out from behind ANTHONY WEINER'S TINY CONSCIENCE. He looks angry.}

THE ALMIGHTY

Since you sent an image of your rod
I've been feeling kind of odd
You were a jackass, let's be clear
But you're not the only problem here
Those who censured you are almost as bad
Opportunists, scolds, they all make me mad
Plus, the Twitter that and the follow this
Something fundamental is amiss
The human race was my first begotten
But now the whole shebang's gone rotten.

ANTHONY WEINER

I said I was sorry
I even got teary
Doesn't that punch
A hole in your theory?

{THE ALMIGHTY ignores ANTHONY WEINER.}

THE ALMIGHTY

I've thought it through and I'm pretty certain
That it's time to bring down the final curtain

Remember back when I made the flood?
This will be like that, but with flames and blood.
Every ocean, boiled. Every city, rubbled.
Till my peaceful rest is no longer troubled.

{THE ALMIGHTY makes good on his promise. It's horrible. All that's left afterward is a gray background, with ANTHONY WEINER'S TINY CONSCIENCE standing in front of it, dazed. Suddenly, HAROLD CAMPING punches through the background.}

HAROLD CAMPING

We're out of time. We're out of jokes.
I told you. Th-th-that's all, folks!

{Fade to black . . . really black.}

SOMEDAY MY CONCESSION SPEECH WILL BE READ BY SCHOOLCHILDREN

Jim Stallard

My friends, this is no time for tears. Tonight is not an ending, but a beginning. When we started this journey together eighteen months ago, nobody could have guessed how much we would shake things up in this country. Though we may have fallen short for now, this is one "laughingstock"—and I wear that label as a badge of honor—who knows the national conversation has changed for the better.

I think we've come to realize that the voters do not yet feel as passionately about typefaces as we do. The pundits said my decision to make "return to the Courier standard" the centerpiece of my campaign was . . . well, what's that word George Will loves to use? "Risible"? I don't even know what that means, and I don't think any of us cares. But like you, I know the day is coming when once again all printed matter—from our laws and ballots to our menus and wedding invitations—will appear in the unpretentious font that is the bedrock of this nation.

You're going to hear a lot tomorrow about the vote totals and how we were beaten by several people running in jest, including the Phillies mascot. But don't despair: game-changing ideas are often rejected at first by the majority. We can take heart from the remark by Gandhi about social movements: "First they ignore you, then they ridicule you, then . . ." I can't remember the rest, but at some point everything works out.

Obviously there were missteps along the way, but we'll be better next time around. Our leaflet drop onto the ceremony at Arlington Cemetery should have been cleared with the authorities. Regarding the now-famous YouTube video from that day on the National Mall—I should have just kissed the baby instead of commenting on its facial proportions. And to the guy who pranked me about the alleged Jim Courier endorsement, leading to our unfortunate e-mail blast: I hope you had some fun with that. I assume you don't care that your proud nation is being emasculated by Helvetica and Poynter.

I see our friendly opposition-research person is still here with that camcorder. "Why does he bother?" you ask. "Doesn't he have enough material?" Well, it's because our opponents are scared of us. They're already thinking four years ahead. I don't deny that I'm a spontaneous guy. And I'm grateful that certain constituencies—the Catholics, the Masons, the Libras, the National Academy of Sciences members, and the 1972 Miami Dolphins—have managed to let go of their anger over my inappropriate remarks. I hope we all can put these incidents behind us and make a better country for our children, one that states its principles in masculine lettering. I'm actually quite close to many Libras; they are a beautiful, childlike people.

As you know, our media gives horse race–type coverage to presidential races rather than focusing on the issues. I became quite frustrated nobody prominent would sit down and let me explain the motivation behind our campaign, or even try to understand how empires can be weakened from within by effete type. My team finally resorted to detaining David Brooks—yes, the thirty-six-hour mystery of his whereabouts is solved—but he somehow made it out of the van when we stopped to use the restroom on our way here. I never got to ask him who the hell Don Quixote is and what he has to do with me.

I expect news of David's escape to hit the airwaves soon, so I need to wrap this up. You should all be proud of what we accomplished.

We've taken the first crucial step in setting this country back on the right track. Now, I'm going to come down from the podium and join with you as we all do the "Courier Cheer" one last time. I look forward to when we'll all be doing it at our inaugural ball.

Never mind, I see the marshals are here.

STARTING OVER WITH PAT NIXON

Tom Gliatto

Ann Landers answered my letter today. "If you are married to the leader of the free world, as you say you are, then are you not one of the free? Or are you one of the led? You see the contradiction inherent in your self-description. Each of us harbors within our hearts the desire to be subjugated and the desire to be liberated. It sounds to me as if it were high time you got off your high horse, lady, and thought all this through. Good luck." This tells me nothing I did not already know. I must and I will break away. My little valise sits at the back of my closet, already packed and waiting for me with a few clothes, a few overnight things. I will move out. Leave the West Wing for the South Wing, abandoned as it is and crumbling, full of cobwebs, rats, and the ghost (or so says the Secret Service) of Mary Todd Lincoln. During rainstorms, she floats through the corridors, mournfully requesting a tarp. RN will not follow me there, or rather he will never get very far. The walls are lined with portraits: Coolidge's children, or at least the ones who survived the booby-trapped sled; Millard Fillmore on his pony, Scamp, with a bachelor friend, also named Scamp; Dolley Madison lounging on an Empire sofa after the fashion of *La Grande Odalisque*. RN will stop and talk to each of them. On and on and on. Then, if he has drunk enough (and he will have drunk enough), he will lapse into patter songs, Gilbert and Sullivan numbers his mother taught him beneath the clementines long ago, when they were both in their mid-thirties.

————

I try to remember when the romance died from our life together, but then I try to remember when the romance actually began, and as I keep searching I go back further and further until I reach a strange, cloudy image of my sister dressed as Santa Claus and swinging wildly at a reindeer piñata. By that point, who knows how many hours have elapsed? An undersecretary of something or other comes in and tells me. Four hours and thirteen minutes, precisely, have elapsed. And now they are back from shopping, RN and Kissinger. Bags from Garfinckel's and Lord & Taylor are flung onto the furniture. (The click of the whiskey decanter being opened, the exchange of limericks that end with "Cambodia.") RN shops to forget, they say, the editorial pages say, the wise men of the *New York Times,* and how long will the public tolerate it? What did it take for the "people" to storm the Bastille? The introduction of a postage-stamp series, "Vacation Spots of the Bourbons." Can it be true that our days here are coming to an end? Deep Throat nods and says, "Oh, yes, yes, it is true, my dear Pat, and then for you—what? What next, I wonder? A delicious question. By the way, did you see there was a letter to Ann Landers from a woman married to the leader of the free world, and Ann told her that one can be free or one can be led? That was followed by a letter from a woman who thought adult diapers from a fiancé was a thoughtless gift. And, Pat, guess what else? Shall I tell you? Ben Bradlee is in love with you. He wants to ride in on a white steed and rescue you. But he knows a white steed won't fit through the White House fence, so he's out in Virginia horse country looking for something slimmer." The light is growing dim inside (outside it unaccountably grows brighter) and I realize, or rather I ask myself, or rather I am saying this out loud: Is it Deep Throat who loves me? Have I loved him all along? Is this the beast in the jungle Mamie Eisenhower was always going on about? It is all too complicated, and I throw him out.

———

Dinner. RN, as always now, is fulminating over injustices perceived and imagined. When were we ever in the Aegean with Armani and Pasolini? Rose Mary, ever-present factotum, loads a tape into the machine, turns it on, and stands back deferentially as RN dictates the evening's menu. He disgusts, disturbs, and vexes me with his compulsive taping. The wind in the trees, Spanish evangelicals on the radio, even the singing of my little canaries. (Are they a metaphor for me, for us? Was it a mistake to name them Patty and Dickie?) Tonight there is so little conversation between us that Rose Mary is assigned to play me. But she has no dramatic imagination and she is quickly reduced to calling out bingo numbers. My own thoughts I resolutely keep to myself. Those are safe, at least, since the Court ruled that the investigative committee cannot subpoena woolgathering, not even if they offer to send over aides with packing material. But I will "spill the beans" once we leave here. I will pick up the phone and call Dick Cavett, or David Frost, or Barbara Walters, whoever happens to be home and close to the phone, and I will offer them my exclusive story, tell them everything. That Checkers, the most artful hoax of RN's early career, was not a spaniel but an oiled poodle. That Haldeman and Ehrlichman were actually Ehrlichman and Haldeman. That we have an imaginary son off at boarding school, and RN and I argue over who is responsible for his lousy test scores. That the only reason we have an enemies list is because we tried to make a list of friends and found we had none.

———

The helicopter lifts off from the White House and flies us out over and down the Potomac, then turns around at Andover, Maryland, and flies us back. RN makes us rehearse the departure again and again, and for what? It's full dress every time, with the press on the lawn, the understudy at his vanity table applying a five o'clock shadow, and the Joint Chiefs of Staff showing off their freshly waxed legs. I am certain now that I will leave RN, strike out on my own. Deep Throat has not yet expressly declared his love to me, although yesterday when we were at Level B in the parking lot he leaked it to me on background. It torments me that I still do not know whether I love him for himself or the fact that his real name is Plácido Domingo. Meanwhile, my mind is whirling with new prospects and projects that promise a glory that I have never known as a politician's wife. Could I, myself, become a politician—a *good* politician in every sense of the word: wise, honest, decent, beloved? No. I cannot fool myself. For years I have rented an office, and yet I know I will never have the courage to run for it. Besides, so many other ideas have accumulated in my mind. For instance, I think you could use aromas and fragrances as a form of emotional therapy. I gave RN a sachet of lavender once. He sniffed it with his long nose and walked away. But he nodded in a way that indicated some fleeting moment of happiness.

HOW YOU VOTED

Jonathan Stern

According to the latest *Park Slope Food Coop Newsletter* / Hot 97 news poll of 1,800 likely voters, Americans are divided on many of the issues under debate today.

When it comes to Wall Street, Americans seem less concerned by *how much* they're getting screwed than by the exact manner of the screwing. More than six in ten Americans said they preferred to lose their savings via declining home values, while the rest were evenly split among stock price overvaluation, Ponzi schemes, health plan deductibles, and being slowly bled dry by tiny bank fees.

When asked what you would do if, hypothetically, you had the power of invisibility and wouldn't get caught, 19 percent of you said you would shoot Dick Cheney, 21 percent of you would watch your child's babysitter take a shower, 22 percent of you would, inexplicably, sit in on a table read for *Whitney,* and a whopping 38 percent of you would watch Dick Cheney take a shower while he watches *Whitney.*

By a ratio of more than three to one, Americans said they were naming their babies Elijah if a boy and Chloe if a girl.

While only 46 percent of Americans believed in the existence of space aliens, more than half of all respondents identified themselves as "either Latino, Black, Asian, or Space Alien," meaning there's a high probability of space aliens living amongst us.

Tax policy was a rare area of common ground. While Republicans and Democrats differed sharply on the issue of capital gains, four out of five males of both parties agreed that college girls who go topless on the beach should be eligible for a tax deduction, while also standing in accord that taxes should be *increased* on those women who *don't* go topless.

There were signs that last summer's opinions on Congress are shifting. In the previous poll, 35 percent described Congress as "a bunch of fucking assholes," 28 percent as "tremendous cocksuckers," and 37 percent as "the kind of people who, if I had a dick, should suck it repeatedly." More recently, however, the numbers were 29 percent for "they were fucking assholes a year ago and they're still fucking assholes now." Eighteen percent said "I *do* have a dick and I really don't want them to actually suck it." Nine percent reported that "my congressman actually did suck my dick in an airport restroom, and you know what? It wasn't that great." Plus, a new group of 44 percent categorized Congress as "*spectacular* cocksuckers."

Overall numbers stayed consistent from previous polls, with 45 percent answering "yes," 29 percent "no," and 26 percent "don't know."

A record 92 percent of adults agreed that pedophiles should be banned from a one-mile radius around school zones, while, in contrast, 8 percent felt that pedophiles should be "specifically invited to stand right outside the school grounds all day, watching."

While some of you felt that the quantity of polls was "just right," 70 percent wanted "to be called every night at dinner, especially for pointless follow-up questions." (The margin of sampling error due to sarcasm is 70 percent.)

Respondents expressed ambivalence about House Congressional proposal H.R. 119, regarding the definition of the fiscal year for certain Ways and Means Committee operating expenses. Surprisingly, there was no strong consensus on this one.

One of the surprisingly fulfilling aspects of my job is to get to know so many people I would never talk to otherwise. It's interesting how many assumptions you make about someone just from their voice turn out to be totally wrong. Really fascinating.

For all the unhappiness about the country's direction, most citizens would still rather be in prison here than anywhere else. Whether the prison is a literal one, like the famed Sing Sing in upstate New York, or more figurative, like junior high, compulsive behavior, a bad marriage, or a dead-end job as a poll analyst, America is still the gold standard in incarceration and hopelessness by a whopping four-to-one margin.

30 AND PREGNANT

Rachel Friedman

"What are you going to do?" my friend Kate whispered across the square table at Le Pain Quotidien. She squeezed my hand.

"I have no idea," I said. I could feel tears collecting in the corners of my eyes. I would not cry in public. I would not. *This is all a bad dream,* I tried to tell myself.

There were several people to break the news to, first and foremost my husband. We've only been married for four years, practically newlyweds! This wasn't part of the plan.

"You're . . . pregnant?" he said when I told him over pasta primavera that evening. "Are you sure?" He eyed me warily. "Is it mine?"

"Of course it's yours!" I cried. What a cretin. He was all sweet talk during our monthly "dates" and here he was in the sober light of day throwing around accusations.

"How did this happen?" he said. I couldn't believe he didn't know. "We were so careful." I sighed heavily, twirling a piece of spaghetti around my fork, feeling overwhelmed that now I would officially have to come down on one side of the cloth-versus-disposable-diapers debate. "Well, of course I'll do my part," he announced in what I assume he thought was a chivalrous tone. "I'll step up to the plate." He reached for his iPhone. "I can't promise that we'll be able to get into a decent pre-K this late in the game, but my colleague's wife is a teacher at the 92nd Street Y. It's worth a shot."

He exchanged some pleasantries with the man on the other end of the line, then mouthed to me, "How far along are you?" He nodded efficiently and scribbled my response on a scrap of paper next to a list of the city's most prestigious schools that he had begun compiling.

Next on the list was my father, the professor. There was a long silence after I confessed to him.

"But you haven't even made tenure yet!" he wailed once he was finally able to speak. "A baby is going to derail your entire career!"

"It's going to be okay, Dad," I said, trying to calm him. "I'll only have to take a few weeks off."

"I thought you were waiting until thirty-five," he said. "That's what good girls do."

"Sometimes accidents happen," I said.

"Try to place at least three articles before the due date," he counseled. "And promise me you'll network extra hard at MLA this year. Wear something loose and no one will even know. You know how people gossip, and you don't want this getting around school."

"A baby?" my mother said. Her eyes were all judgment. "Why would you want to do such a thing?" She poured balsamic vinegar on her salad and beckoned the waiter over for more lemons. "You completely ruined my figure, not to mention my marriage."

"I'm sorry," I said.

"Do you know how much Pilates you're going to have to do after all this"—here she motioned with an open palm toward my still-flat stomach—"is said and done?"

"I can handle it," I said.

"That's what they all say," she said. "You have no idea how much work it is." She squeezed the fresh lemon into her water and bit into the rind. "Staying thin is a full-time job, and anyone who says differently is lying."

My friends were, of course, extremely concerned for me. How was I going to raise a kid at my age? I was practically a kid myself! It wasn't going to be easy, that much I knew. I'd seen the reality shows: *Mid-Career and Pregnant, Still Renting and Pregnant, An Undiversified Portfolio and Pregnant*. I didn't *have* to have this child. There were options, options I did not want to think about, but options nonetheless. I had my whole life ahead of me, after all. Should I really be asked to sacrifice everything because of this one mistake? I put a hand on my stomach, hoping the creature inside would give me some answers. *Am I ready for the suburbs?* I asked, like it was a Magic 8 Ball. *Am I ready for bulk shopping at Costco? Am I ready for negotiating vacation days with nannies? Am I ready to give up sushi?*

No answers were forthcoming.

I'M AFRAID THE CHILDREN
ARE OUR FUTURE

John Moe

I'm seeing them again this election season. Little headlines in parenting magazines, mentions in the preschool newsletter, even casual comments in the e-mails of friends who have small kids. "Vote for your children," they say, or "Vote for kids!" or "Cast your ballot for the future generation." I know they mean well. All they want is for this country to be a good place for our youngsters, clean environment and quality schools or whatever. But they have no idea what a dangerous game they're playing.

Two years ago I was like these people. My son, Pete, was four years old and my daughter, Lucy, had just turned two. I wanted them to have every opportunity in life, and I thought it not just important but crucial for me to campaign on their behalf. "I'm voting for my kids," I'd say to anyone who would listen. "I'm casting my vote with Pete and Lucy in mind." How could I have expected what happened?

As all voters know, a lot of people heard me back then and overwhelmingly agreed with my sentiment. Lucy won an unexpected majority of votes, all write-in, and was elected to the U.S. House of Representatives. Four-year-old Pete, meanwhile, was declared the surprise winner of the vacant Senate seat at nine-fifteen that night, an hour after passing out during yet another viewing of his well-worn *Dora the Explorer* videocassette. Without ever knowing that they had run, and without even knowing what the institution was, my kids were members of Congress.

Breakfast the next morning was awkward, as we tried to convince the kids to eat their scrambled eggs and fruit even while they fielded questions from the crew of reporters that had waited in our carport all night (no, we told the news crews, we won't wake up the newly elected). Within days, my wife and I had quit our jobs and were toting the two sleepiest and crankiest new policymakers in Washington around D.C., trying to find a decent apartment within stroller range of their offices. As we waded through résumés and were beset by lobbyists while trying to assemble not one but two congressional staffs, my wife would often repeat my words back to me in a harsh and mocking tone: "Vote for the kids," she'd say, shrilly; "*I'm* voting for *my* kids!" Her acrimony was deserved.

I must admit that even knowing them as I did, I held out hope that the kids would accomplish something. Sure, I had seen stubborn refusals to take baths, violent reactions to an improperly cut sandwich, and hysterical fits based on the necessity of leaving a given playground. None of those bode well for a career in public service, I knew that, but maybe the kids' innocence and lack of guile would actually be a plus, since they were beholden to no one and incapable of animosity. Did they quarrel? Sure, but it never turned into lingering grudges. Plus, I suspected they were both geniuses, although that's just a dad thing.

Of course, the disastrous consequences of Lucy's first term and the first two years of Pete's are matters of public and congressional record, and have been well chronicled, scathingly so, in our local papers. Pete's legislative failures include the ill-advised "I Want to Be a Stegosaurus" bill, the doomed "How About a Purple Floating House That Eats Space?" legislation, and the notorious "Everyone Should Have Fourteen Dogs" plan that, despite getting some support from a few niche industries, was roundly and justly ridiculed long before it reached the floor. His tenure almost ended abruptly when a new dump truck presented by a crafty NRA lobbyist very nearly resulted in the most dramatic rollback of gun-control laws this country has ever seen. Pete got off with a public rebuke and a long "time out" for that one, although what was left of his political credibility was destroyed. Not that the senator cared.

Lucy's performance, if this is even possible, was worse. While other members of the House were positioning themselves on committees and trying to serve their constituencies, two-year-old Representative Lucy mostly stayed in her office, repeatedly putting the yarn-haired doll to "bed" while demanding that her staff read her *Barney Goes to the Pet Shop*. Again. Votes during session were even more embarrassing, as Lucy pretty much mimicked the vote of whoever was sitting next to her. Over time, House members looking to score one extra crucial vote would try to sit next to Lucy, partially to gain her vote but also, I suspect, because they kind of liked having her cuddle up in their lap. While Lucy amassed an increasingly opulent dollhouse empire, thanks to moneyed political action committees, companies packed up and moved out of her district, incurring not the slightest objection from Washington. Needless to say, neither Lucy nor her brother Pete did a thing to help the cause of children in general, aside from the fleet of ponies that were unexpectedly appointed to Pete's old daycare.

So now it's two years later. Maybe Pete will be ready for reelection when he's ten years old and his term expires, although I'm certain he'll do nothing in the next four years to deserve anyone's votes, especially now that he's discovered the Power Rangers. But I do know I'll be voting for almost anyone before I vote for Lucy. Not only is she the most incompetent representative our district has ever had, but Ms. Deana says she looks tired and unfocused in preschool. As Election Day looms, voters are again being told to "vote for our kids." I say, fine. Go ahead, vote for your kids. Just please don't vote for mine.

HOW SUPERIOR EACH BAR FEELS TO THE OTHERS

Ben Greenman

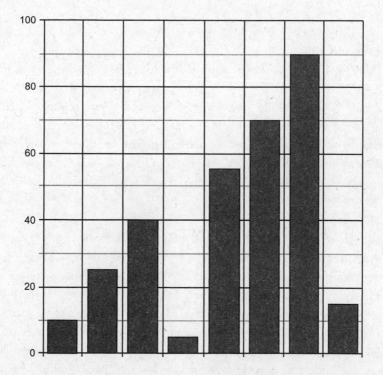

CLASSIC NURSERY RHYMES, UPDATED AND REVAMPED FOR THE RECESSION, AS TOLD TO ME BY MY FATHER

Jen Statsky

Jack and Jill

Okay, so Jack and Jill went up the hill to fetch a pail of water. But, listen, even water is expensive nowadays. So Jack just innocently asked, "Do you really have to wash your hair *every* night?" Then, of course, they started getting into it, and Jill became pretty damn passive-aggressive, and unnecessarily, I might add. So then Jack fell down—maybe on accident, maybe on purpose—and he broke his crown. And, with no health insurance, they were both shit outta luck.

Humpty Dumpty

Sure, in a perfect world, we'd all help put Humpty Dumpty back together, whether we were on the king's payroll or not. There's no question about that. But the world isn't lilacs and lollipops anymore, kid. I can barely afford all your mother's pill . . . pillows, all the pillows she insists on sleeping with at night. So, if there's some sort of freak accident with a wall? Forget about it. But everyone needs to take a certain level of responsibility for themselves in a time like this, and let's face it: Humpty was carrying—what, twenty, thirty extra el-bees on him? That's just reckless. I don't care if you are the king, you can't cover that premium and sleep easy at night.

Old Mother Hubbard

If you want to talk about being irresponsible, this Mother Hubbard is the Cadillac of not thinking about anyone but herself. What is this old woman doing owning a pet in this economy in the first place? You know she's tearing through her retirement funds like nobody's business, so of course her cupboards are bare, cupboards that are probably made of mahogany with gold-plated handles, since people believed in unicorns before they believed that this bubble would ever pop. But, okay, it doesn't all fall on her. Where are her kids? You work hard to raise children, set them up nice in the world, and once times get a little tougher than usual they abandon you. Well, I feel sorry for that damn dog. He's the only innocent one in this whole stinkin' mess.

Twinkle, Twinkle, Little Star

"Twinkle, twinkle, little star, how I wonder what you are. Up above the world so high, like a diamond in the sky . . . ." Ha! A diamond. Give me a break. The only place anyone's going to see a diamond nowadays is in a geometry book. And, if some guy proposes to you and shows you some ring with a shiny rock, you run the other way. And fast. Like a gazelle. Because he's mixed up in some kind of silly racket, let me tell you.

Jack Be Nimble

Jack is clearly on drugs. And, sure, the temptation to do some uppers and escape from all this lousy stuff is there. I'm not immune to that; I'm a human being. But, honey, look where it gets you. You spend your days jumping over some candlestick like some sort of circus monkey, but who's taking care of your family? Jack's probably got three kids wearing Ziploc bags for mittens and banging pots and pans on the subway to make a dime. It just ain't right.

Rock-a-Bye Baby

It's sick, it's freakin' sick, honey. I couldn't hold down a tuna melt for days after hearing this one. But it's the sad truth in times like these. People get desperate, they don't know what to do or where to turn, and they do twisted things, like putting some poor defenseless baby up on a rickety tree branch. Priorities, that's the real problem here. People get their priorities all out of whack, and we end up in a situation like this. Why did they need some fancy rocking cradle in the first place? People get so caught up with image they never stop to think that maybe that poor little kid would have rather just been held in his or her own parents' arms, instead of some high-tech Sears and Roebuck baby palace.

Little Bo Peep

Now, I didn't do none of that collegiate stuff that everyone does nowadays, which I think was the start of this whole mess in the first place, but I'm pretty sure the lost sheep are meant to symbolize hope, promise, and, more specifically, the American Dream. I like that part, I do. You can relate to it. But then this Bo Peep chick falls asleep, and at first I said, "Whoa there. Are you trying to say that Americans collectively took a nap at the wheel of the vehicle of their own success and prosperity?" Harsh stuff. But then I thought more about it, and you know what? That's exactly what we did. And, sure, we were following the crooked street signs put up by the banks and investment firms, but that's no excuse to go on autopilot. So, you know, I like this Bo Peep one very much.

There Was an Old Woman Who Lived in a Shoe

Yep, sounds about right to me. But, for the love of God, use a rubber.

THE ADVENTURES OF RIGHT-WING CONSERVATIVE ROBIN HOOD

Sarah Rosenshine

Giving an account of Right-Wing Conservative Robin Hood and his Merry Men, who gave to the rich, and let it trickle down to the poor.

———

IN A MERRY COUNTRY in the time of old, when good King Reagan ruled the land, there lived near Nottingham Township a famous man whose name was Robin Hood. He lived within the green glades of Sherwood Forest, Sherwood Forest being the name of a gated community. He was an archer the likes of which had never been seen, because he only arched occasionally in the privacy of his expansive backyard. Right happily he dwelt within the walls of Sherwood Forest, suffering neither care nor want but passing the time in games of croquet or pin-the-tail-on-the-serving-maid and living upon venison, washed down with draughts of ale of October brewing, or so he was told by the man who bought his beer for him.

Not only Robin himself but all his band of Merry Men dwelt apart from others, as Sherwood Forest was six miles outside of town and only accessible by a single winding road, which itself was punctuated by several large electrified gates, built to keep out deer and poor people. Yet on occasion, a brave soul risked electrocution to come ask Robin for venison to feed his children, and it was then that noble Robin would refuse him meat. And if he asked for drink to quench his thirst, Robin would refuse him draught. And if he asked for cloth to clothe his family, Robin would refuse him wool. But just as the man would turn to leave, Robin would place his hand upon the man's shoulder, and assure him that when the new open-air market finally opened in six months and the new pub a year after that, Robin would frequent these establishments, and then they would expand, and maybe then the man at his door could get a job there and his family would no longer go hungry. And when Robin was asked to explain how that made any sense at all, he would say he had to go hunting.

Then the man would take this promise home to his children, and it would fill their tiny hearts, though not their equally tiny bellies.

Now I will tell you how it came about that Robin Hood fell afoul of the law.

When Robin was a man of forty-eight, large of stomach and of mouth, he grew restless. And the restlessness grew and grew until one day bold Robin stopped paying his taxes completely, because he was weary of his money going to the government and not into his own bank account, where it would sit forever. Instead, Robin gave this money to the rich, and told them, "Invest it in your businesses!" And the rich took the money and put it in their bank accounts, where it sat forever. But everyone felt good about themselves, and Robin assumed the poor did, too, because they did not say anything.

Then the Sheriff of Nottingham Township was filled with rage, for he needed the money to keep the streets clean and the libraries stocked and the public schools open, but Robin did not want to pay for these services, because the children he had with Maid Marian did not even attend public schools, and why should his ample gold go toward them at all?

So Robin proposed a round of golf on Sherwood Forest's unparalleled course, and he invited the Sheriff, and he offered to the Sheriff hors d'oeuvres and cheese and enough wine to put a small horse to sleep, and then he and the Sheriff were great friends, and soon the taxes were "no longer a problem."

And everyone that mattered lived happily ever after.

TWO MEDIEVAL PHYSICIANS DEBATE UNIVERSAL HEALTH CARE

Blair Becker

HASTINGS: You know, Gaunt, I'm glad we were both scheduled to drive the plague cart today. There's something I've been meaning to ask you: What's your professional opinion of this universal-health-care business?

GAUNT: I'll tell you right now—it stinks like a smallpox boil. You can heat it, cool it, or lance it, but it's not going away. And we really stand to take a hit in our share of this barter-based economy.

HASTINGS: Yeah, yeah, I know all that. But wouldn't you rather have slightly fewer sides of half-rotted beef in your larder if it meant everyone could have access to someone like you or me?

GAUNT: Oh Heavenly Father, if you don't sound like the Thomas Becket of barbers! Have you learned nothing since our altruistic five days of medical school? Forget the poor. They are more likely to get diphtheria and die anyway. Medicine should be ruled by the same feudal market forces that determine all other services. If you don't produce your quota, then you'll die by the disemboweling scoop at home rather than by the sword in battle. Remember, seven minutes per paying patient.

HASTINGS: I can't believe I'm hearing this from the guy who used to talk about running free clinics in the peasant quarter. Remember when we used to say that restoring the four humors was all the payment we needed?

GAUNT: Listen, ever since I decided to subspecialize and take that residency in leechology, I have been raking in the livestock and cordwood. I've got a nice private practice in the hamlet out east, and I bleed them all dry. The malpractice insurance isn't bad, either—I just pay a neighborhood kid to drop pertussis in the butter churn if any of my patients start complaining. Hey, I couldn't cure that stuff if I wanted to! You've got to look out for number one, Hastings. With the lawyers going the way they are, they'll soon be suing us for keeping all the lepers together. You and I both know that like cures like, but you just can't explain science to some people.

HASTINGS: I know our colleagues don't put a lot of stock in "outcomes," but I just keep thinking about the one patient I've saved in my twenty years of practice. Though we are centuries away from developing anesthesia, it felt good to cut off his healthy leg, knowing that it would teach his crippled leg to straighten out. Call me naive, but I truly believe that everyone deserves to be bled or sweated when they're at death's door, regardless of the feudal position they're born into. Everyone has the right to be healthy enough to one day suffer a violent death.

GAUNT: I, unfortunately, haven't been taught to harbor an angry sense of skepticism when it comes to socialist propaganda, Hastings, but I do know that I understand the concept of taking care of the caregiver. When I shuttle the patrician class out of the city during the summer epidemics and lock them in rooms with blazing fires and garlic compresses, I know that they pay me handsomely for their torment. Quite frankly, I don't want to give that up. So go ahead and see how far this talk of "rights" and "Parliament" takes you, but for now I'm resolved to provide universal health care for those who can pay me. At this rate, you will probably die of cholera while tending to some mead addict on charity from the church. But if you want to deal with the terrible reimbursement and papal oversight, no one is going to stop you.

HASTINGS: Fair enough, Doc. I feel like I'm kind of losing steam on this issue, anyway. I tend to speak inspirationally about progressive change, but then inevitably fail to implement it. It's also an election year for the Medical Society and I've been getting a lot of donations from Big Herbal.

THE TWENTY-FIRST CENTURY
ADVENTURES OF TINTIN

Neil Graf

Tintin Interferes in the Georgian Election

Tintin in Darfur

Tintin Blames America First

Prescription Drugs of the Canadians

The Chinese Environmental Nightmare

The Venezuelan Tin Ear

President Milošević's Sceptre

*The Ecstasy Being Smuggled by American Servicemen in the Persian Gulf
Is Packed in Cigars Imprinted with the Crab with the Golden Claws*

The Secret of UNESCO

Somali Pirates' Treasure

The Seven-Crystal Meth

Prisoners in Guantánamo

Land of Iraqi Gold

Destination Reverend Moon's Congressional Influence

Explorers Flipping Over Because of Faulty Firestone Tires

The Bordurians Kicked Out the Weapons Inspectors After the Calculus Affair and Now We Will Have to Disarm Them

The Iranian Speedboat Sharks

Tintin Parties at the Everest Base Camp

The Gypsies Did Not Actually Steal the Emerald

Hi, I'm Captain John Travolta, Welcome to Flight 714

Tintin and the Zapatistas

Tintin Doesn't Understand Art

YOUTH CULTURE FINDINGS

Dan Kennedy

Someone born in 1990 has never seen MTV as a music channel or as a destination for music knowledge or information, and has never watched a movie in a movie theater. Or seen a stove.

The average teenager today is engaged in sexual activity with at least two different partners for about seventy-two hours per week. And you can double that figure—for both cumulative time and number of partners—when LSD rave parties come into the picture.

A baby born this year will be controlled by tiny radios by the time it's eleven.

Teenagers rarely use telephones to communicate with their friends anymore; if they want to talk to someone, they'll just meet people in witch cults in the mountains outside Olympia, Washington. Cell-phone service providers generally frustrate them, so they resort to making drugs or breaking into homes that appear to be vacant.

Teenaged girls most identify with—and aspire to be similar to—singer-songwriter Sting, and enjoy using marking pens to write the phrase "Pee or fart on me" on unconscious peers.

The average American child today has, by the age of twelve, tried marijuana at least once. By age thirteen, that same child has sold clean urine and the retinas of cadavers to spies, then committed suicide.

Eighty percent of the teenagers we spoke with admitted to performing street theater in blackface, usually spitballing and showboating with a straight man or an "easy mark" audience plant.

Teenagers often affectionately greet adults with the phrase "Twat did you say?"—which, loosely translated, is taken to mean "You're okay with me. You're in the club."

APRIL FOOLS' DAY PRANKS TO PLAY ON AN UNEMPLOYED TWENTYSOMETHING MALE WHO STILL LIVES AT HOME WITH HIS PARENTS

Christopher Monks

Take a hammer to his Xbox.

Drop a cinder block on his Xbox.

Drive your station wagon over his Xbox.

Buy him a new Xbox, then smash his old Xbox with his new Xbox.

Prepare his favorite meal. Over dinner, tell him that no matter how hard things might seem right now, you will always be there for him. Then set fire to his Xbox.

YOUR PROTEST SIGNS ARE TOO SPECIFIC

Alan Trotter

MARRIAGE = 1 MAN + 1 WOMAN but after all these wonderful years together I'm glad we decided to invite a third party, someone we both knew and trusted, into our bedroom. It was great and only made me better appreciate how much I LOVE YOU HONEY.

———

I AM PRO-CHOICE BUT if someone gave me the choice of pressing a button and I'd get a million dollars except a stranger would die—like in that movie?—MAN I DON'T KNOW WHAT I WOULD DO . . .

———

It's Adam and Eve NOT Adam and Lucy, who always did everything she could to make me feel insignificant.

———

NO BLOOD FOR Oh crap I just remembered I need to buy some olive oil. And come to think of it, it's been years since I last gave blood. It's not like it takes long, and they always need all that they can get—people should really think of it as a civic duty, but here I am and I can't even remember the last time I went. Today, though, right after this: gonna go, give blood, get a free biscuit. BRING OUR TROOPS HOME.

———

Keep your laws OFF MY BODY! But don't stop running your fingers through my hair or whispering to me with your hot, dirty mouth pressed against my ear, you sexy senator you.

LESS POWERFUL INDUSTRY LOBBYING GROUPS

Todd Rovak

Big Cartography

Big Orange Julius

Smaller Tobacco

Really, Nothing to Sneeze At Oil

Slightly Less Imposing Pharma

My Mother and Her Letter-Writing

National Association of People Who Pretty Much Keep Their Feelings All Bottled Up Inside

U.S. Federation of Nonvoters Without Money

Stray Dogs for a Free Tibet

FRAGMENTS FROM *PALIN! THE MUSICAL*

Ben Greenman

Premiered: December 19, 2012
Performances: 114
Note: *On opening night, the celebrities in the crowd included Josh Groban, Ryan Gosling, Joan Rivers, and Mia Hamm. Glen Rice was not in attendance.*

───────

{It is 2007. Alaska governor SARAH PALIN is taking a rare afternoon off from work. She walks by a strip mall. Like all Alaskan strip malls, it contains a moose-supply store, a pizza parlor, and a doctor's office. She stops to admire the moose-supply store window and almost bumps into a DOCTOR.}

DOCTOR

Hello. I'm an obstetrician.

SARAH PALIN

Well, hello. I'm a politician.

DOCTOR

Good day, madam.

SARAH PALIN

Good day, sir.
I'm not pregnant.

DOCTOR

Who said you were?

{A few days later, SARAH PALIN returns to the doctor's office.}

SARAH PALIN

I've been so busy
With governance
That I've neglected
To be inspected.
I'd like to have an exam now, please.

DOCTOR

Get on the table and raise your knees.

{The DOCTOR determines that SARAH PALIN is pregnant.}

SARAH PALIN

Holy moly!
Sakes alive!
I have four kids.
This makes five.

{A few months later, SARAH PALIN is at a conference.}

SARAH PALIN

We need to make the country work
For ordinary folk.
Direct reform must be the norm,
And . . . Oops, my water broke.

{*SARAH PALIN flies home to Alaska to have the baby.*}

SARAH PALIN

We'll call him Trig.
It means "strength" in Norse.
We'll care for him, raise him,
And love him, of course.

{*SARAH PALIN continues to govern the state, tend to her family, help her husband with his business, and find time for herself.*}

SARAH PALIN

Take that, Murkowski!
It's dinnertime, kids!
Goodbye, Bridge to Nowhere!
Hello, dogsled skids!
Need haircut, need yoga!
Need food for the house!
Need to remember
To pick up that blouse!
Drill here, drill now!
No, not you, Todd!
An hour till hockey,
Then the Iditarod.

{*One afternoon, SARAH PALIN's teenaged daughter BRISTOL PALIN approaches her.*}

BRISTOL PALIN

Mom,
We have to talk.

SARAH PALIN

Come with me
While I walk.
The guys at work all call it
My morning constitutional.
That's what passes for a joke.
Politics is institutional.

BRISTOL PALIN

Mom,
I think I'm late.

{SARAH PALIN's phone rings.}

SARAH PALIN

One second.
In this state,
Where ethical breaches
And pork-filled bills are legion,
We need a real reformer
To rectify the region.

BRISTOL PALIN

Mom,
I need you now.

SARAH PALIN

My schedule

Won't allow
A heart-to-heart till Thursday.

BRISTOL PALIN

Mom, listen, I'm pregnant!

SARAH PALIN

Well, now I'm *bouleversée*.
I think of you as a child still, a
Tomboy on the loose in Wasilla,
Though I see that you are a woman now.
We have to fix this soon. But how?

{SARAH PALIN visits her daughter's boyfriend, LEVI JOHNSTON. As she approaches him, she hears him bragging to his friends.}

LEVI JOHNSTON

I shot, I scored.
The puck is in the goal.
I shot, I scored.
We didn't practice birth control,
Or gun control, for that matter.
Easy-Bake Oven, meet baby batter.
I may have mixed a metaphor,
But what do I care?
I shoot, I score!

{SARAH PALIN clears her throat. LEVI JOHNSTON turns to see the governor standing beside him.}

SARAH PALIN

I hunt with a shotgun,
Not a musket or pistol.

I'm holding one now.
Will you marry my Bristol?

LEVI JOHNSTON

I'm an effing redneck, ma'am.
It says so on my MySpace page.
I'm not sure I can marry her,
Because, well, we're both underage.

SARAH PALIN

You two can marry.
We'll have a wedding.
Otherwise, it'll be
You I'm beheading.
I'll come down on you like an atom bomb.

LEVI JOHNSTON

Well, uh, I mean, can I call you Mom?

{Across the country, JOHN McCAIN is meeting with CHARLIE BLACK and RICK DAVIS to decide whom to pick for vice president.}

JOHN McCAIN

I think I want
Joe Lieberman.

CHARLIE BLACK

With him, there's no way
You can win.

JOHN McCAIN

Well, what about Tom Ridge instead?

CHARLIE BLACK

Do that and your campaign is dead.

RICK DAVIS

We need a conservative who can serve.

JOHN McCAIN

You jerks are getting on my last nerve.

{The phone rings in the Palin home.}

TODD PALIN

Sarah, phone.
It's John McCain.

SARAH PALIN

The guy from *Die Hard*?
I love that movie.

TODD PALIN

No, the senator.

SARAH PALIN

Oh, okay. Groovy.

{JOHN McCAIN offers her a spot on the Republican ticket.}

JOHN McCAIN

Is there anything
I need to know
About your family?

SARAH PALIN

No. Although,
Now that you mention it,
Once, back in the eighties,
Todd was driving tipsy
And dinged up a Mercedes.

JOHN McCAIN

You sure
That's all?

SARAH PALIN

That's all
I recall.

JOHN McCAIN

That's really
Quite small.
Excellent. You've got the job.
Rick and Charlie can polish my knob.

{McCAIN picks her. Though the Obama campaign does not criticize SARAH PALIN directly, they dispatch an army of winged, fanged DEMO-CRATIC OPERATIVES to do so.}

DEMOCRATIC OPERATIVE #1

How can she
Care for her infant son
And also help
The country run?

DEMOCRATIC OPERATIVE #2

The baby's not hers.
It belongs to her daughter.
The water that broke
Wasn't really her water.

DEMOCRATIC OPERATIVE #3

She's like a spy
Working in our midst,
A hot one who is
A separatist.

DEMOCRATIC OPERATIVE #4

The University
Of Idaho?
Where is that, even?
I don't know.

{SARAH PALIN issues a folksy response.}

SARAH PALIN

Come on, that's just not fair of you.
I'm going to hunt caribou.
Then I'll go for stag. Then I'll go for bear.
Corrupt politicians should also beware.
I'm locked. I'm loaded.
D.C.'s outmoded.
The old way's dying.
The underlying
Causes are too great to number.
For starters, power makes you dumber.
It tends to encumber the heart and the spirit.
Silence your inner voice until you can't hear it.

That's what's happening, you see,
To the Democratic nominee.
I won't do that. Don't forget
I auctioned off a private jet.
I'll listen to myself.
I'll listen to my Lord.
I'll listen to my family.
And we will be restored.

{JOHN McCAIN is moved by her straight talk and her reformer's instinct, as are her opponents in the election, BARACK OBAMA and JOE BIDEN. Despite that, JOHN McCAIN and SARAH PALIN are defeated handily. SARAH PALIN regroups by stepping down from office.}

SARAH PALIN

I don't want to govern anymore
That's not what governor is for
I mean, it is, but I'm not it
Never say die. Just say, "I quit."

{SARAH PALIN is hired by Fox News as an analyst and also stars in a reality show about Alaska. Along the way, she becomes a spokesperson for the burgeoning Tea Party.}

SARAH PALIN

It's not a party. We don't have tea.
But it keeps me on TV.

{In the 2012 election, SARAH PALIN decides not to run for president, due in part to the rise of conservative star MICHELE BACHMANN, another Tea Party favorite.}

MICHELE BACHMANN

I hear you talking in my ear.
Where's the camera? Over here?
Okay. I need to tell the nation
About my growing consternation
With President No-Jobs-and-Freedom
We have to all rise up and beat him
At the polls, I mean, of course,
Not beat him like he's a dead horse.
Oh my, he's not a horse at all . . .
Or dead . . .

{MICHELE BACHMANN blanches.}

MICHELE BACHMANN

I have to take a call.

{SARAH PALIN enjoys her relatively private life of ceaseless grandstanding, apart from the hundreds of hours when she is on television. MICHELE BACHMANN remains in the race for the GOP nomination, dropping out after poor showings in consecutive primaries. She eventually loses the nomination to MEWT SANTORICH, a laboratory hybrid created by accident when former Massachusetts governor Mitt Romney and former Pennsylvania senator Rick Santorum are visiting a research facility and are distracted by former Speaker of the House Newt Gingrich, whose white hair reminds them of a Fisher-Price Little Person. Romney and Santorum, in hysterics, fail to notice an iron stairway. They tumble the length of it into a vat of a solution that the researchers affectionately refer to as "DNA Superglue." Gingrich, worried about being left out, jumps in after them. The resulting creature can utter only four phrases, including "I balanced the budget" and "I'm not going to apologize for being successful," but he is very handsome, and he narrowly defeats BARACK OBAMA for the presidency. MEWT SANTORICH calls SARAH PALIN to ask her to join his cabinet, but she is busy pitching

a new TV show, Kate Plus Eight: Now With Less Kate, *in which she
and* TODD PALIN *are trying to raise their new octuplets: Todd Jr., Haley,
Window, Windsor, Gossamer, Potpourri, Shemp, and Todd Jr. Jr.}*

MEWT SANTORICH

That is absurd, in the extreme.
I wish you luck, though. Ponzi scheme.

SARAH PALIN

And good luck to you too, sir.
I'm sure you will be fine.
And you know where to find me:
Thursday nights on TLC, at nine.

MARXIST-SOCIALIST JOKES

Jesse Eisenberg

Why did the Marxist-Socialist cross the road?
To get to the Marxist-Socialist sit-in on the other side of the road.

———

How many Marxist-Socialists does it take to screw in a light-bulb?
Two: one to screw in the light bulb and one to lament Milton Friedman's laissez-faire economic policies.

———

A Marxist-Socialist walks into a bar and asks the bartender if he's unionized.

———

Knock knock.
Who's there?
A Marxist-Socialist.
A Marxist-Socialist who?

A Marxist-Socialist who wants to give you a pamphlet about class struggle.

––––––

What did one Marxist-Socialist say to another?
Like you, I also advocate a proletarian revolution culminating in collective ownership.

––––––

What do you get when you cross a Marxist with a Socialist?
Two people who generally feel that the value of a commodity is equal to its socially necessary labor time.

––––––

What's the difference between a Marxist-Socialist and a Keynesian economist?
Several things, including but not limited to the following: The Marxist-Socialist believes that workers should own the means of production, whereas Keynesians support private ownership over the means of production. Marxist-Socialists believe that centralized government would ultimately wither away after a revolution, whereas Keynesians advocate greater government action to ensure full societal employment. Finally, a Marxist-Socialist would not be invited to a party that a Keynesian was throwing at work because the Keynesian knows that the Marxist-Socialist would throw a stink about the way the cubicles in the Keynesian's office are arranged.

––––––

How do you get a one-armed Marxist-Socialist out of a tree?
Ask two teamsters to drive three AFL-CIO riggers each carrying an

IAFF-approved ladder to the tree and help the one-armed Marxist-Socialist down.

———

The Marxist-Socialist's mother is so fat that when the Marxist-Socialist's mother laments stagflation, she *actually* stagflates.

———

A priest, a rabbi, and a Marxist-Socialist are in an airplane that is going to crash, and there are only two parachutes. The priest says, "I have always followed the word of Jesus, so I should have one of the parachutes." The rabbi says, "I paid for the plane rental, so I should also have one of the parachutes." The Marxist-Socialist says, "I would normally advocate allocating these out according to one's means, but I'm afraid of dying and would like one of the chutes, please."

WHAT IF GERMANY WON THE WAR?

Mike Sacks

And so it came to pass that President Hitler now ruled this land officially called America-Germany in English and Germany-America in
German, the official language.

President Hitler was an able leader. And frightening. Because
of this, he was apt to get his way in many areas, most specifically
politics (e.g., the Ruling of August 24, 1951, in which every man,
woman, and child not named Rolf was made to change his or her
name to Ralph).

And yet he was luckless in the way of love. Which is where Marilyn Monroe came into the picture.

"President Hitler, I love you so very much," Marilyn said to the
president one day while the two of them were making love. They had
met a few months earlier, during a convention in Baltimore, Maryland, the new and official capital of Germany-America. (Note: Washington, D.C.—once but a mere swamp—had once again become but
a mere swamp, one of the many swamps that now dotted the land-
scape like spots on a hyena, the new official national animal.)

But that was then . . . and this was now.

The president stood up and lit his pipe. "You're not making
much sense," he said, by way of his special translator.

"The reason that I say as much," said Marilyn, now talking in

German, also by way of special translator, "is that I want to speak to you. I want to talk to you about getting rid of the—"

"The bomb?" finished Hitler, now smoking a cigar and talking without his translator, whom he had just shot. "The nuclear bomb?"

Hitler laughed long and hard. When he was finished, he declared: "My darling, you must understand many things. One of which is that the bomb will never be gotten rid of. Not in this lifetime or the next. Or in any lifetime. Or anytime else."

Marilyn, now beginning to feel less shy, but still completely nude, save for a Christmas hat—last night had been Christmas—made her way over to Hitler.

"My darling," Marilyn said. "Ever since the War of Freedom ended and you kicked Ralph Roosevelt out of office and put him into a dungeon, you have never talked much about the bomb." Marilyn (after speaking) took a deep, frightened breath. She had never spoken this way before. Least of all to Hitler.

"You are correct," said Hitler, lighting a cigarette. "I have waited many years to talk about the bomb. And ever since I became president, I have not talked about it. That is, until now."

President Hitler picked up the special red hotline phone that connected him directly with the prime minister of England, Joseph Stalin. While dialing, Hitler stroked his Nazi flag. It was exactly the same as an American flag, minus the stars and stripes, and with the addition of a swastika.

"Prime Minister of England, I presume?" asked Hitler, nodding quietly to himself and touching the very small Liberty Bell that was sitting on his desk. The bell was in the shape of a World War I Imperial spiked Panzer helmut ("helmet" was spelled incorrectly in Germany-America at this time).

"That would be I," replied Stalin, five thousand miles and a world away. "And what can I do for you, dear sir? Is it about the tennis match that we will soon have in which the winner will win the world?"

Hitler laughed long and hard. When he was finished, he wiped his mouth with his red, white, and blue handkerchief, the one not with the swastika on it, but rather, a green apple. Hitler loved apples, and ever since winning the war, he wanted as many images of green apples as humanly possible. Apples at this time were a symbol of virility and power. They were also Hitler's favorite food.

"That's funny!" said Hitler. "You're a very funny man, Stalin! But, no, the reason for this call has to do with the nuclear bomb. Is now a good time to talk about it?"

Stalin said nothing, and Hitler said nothing in return.

"I'm waiting," said Hitler, interrupting his silence.

"You win," said Stalin. "I will get rid of the bomb, but I want you to promise me something."

"And what would that happen to be?" asked Hitler, about to hang up the phone.

Hitler hung up the phone before Stalin could finish, and lit a pipe. He began to puff.

"Why did you hang up?" asked Marilyn, confused. "I'm perplexed."

"You have many things to learn," said Hitler, walking over to the bed and sitting down. He began to pull off his uniform, but then changed his mind and stood up. He was now nearly nude, save for a giant cowboy hat—at this time, the elite army of Germany-America wore giant cowboy hats—and he had much to say.

"To begin with, you are very beautiful, but you will not always remain so," said Hitler. And then he finished: "So, you see, my darling, without the bomb, there shall be no more wars."

President Hitler lit a cigar. He walked over to the bed and sat down. He was now fully dressed, save for a gold bracelet and a silver chain. The silver chain represented unity and power. Hitler also owned a necklace made out of white gold, which represented companionship and love. Marilyn had bought it for him.

Before the misery.

Before the pain . . .

It had been exactly three months before that night. Marilyn had stood before Hitler, and Hitler had said: "There is no way that I want you to have this baby, Marilyn. There is too much sadness in the world. There is too much heartbreak. I want my baby to live in a world where there is no pain. Where there is no heartbreak."

Marilyn had began to sob and nodded her head. She was in so much pain, and yet she understood exactly what Hitler meant. "There can be no other way," she had said, sitting back down. "No other way. Perhaps another way, but I don't know."

That was exactly three months ago. Nothing had changed since then, minus their increasing respect for each other.

"Exactly," said Marilyn, agreeing.

And so it came to pass that President Hitler now ruled this land officially called "America-Germany" in English and "Germany-America" in German, the official language. And, although there were no more nuclear bombs to be afraid of, there was also no more fear of war. The absence of nuclear bombs took care of that scenario.

It was all ironic: President Hitler was actually a good president! No one could believe it, except for Marilyn, who was now pregnant with another one of his babies—who would soon grow up to also rule the world. The baby's name?

Ralph Hitler.

METROID'S SAMUS ARAN SPEAKS OUT ABOUT GAY MARRIAGE

Marco Kaye

My upbringing was nontraditional, to say the least. Orphaned as a young child, after a dragon named Ridley slaughtered my parents, I was brought up on the planet Zebes by an alien race known as the Chozo. Half-bird and half-human, my Chozo surrogates taught me that gender, relationships, and sexuality do not follow rigid rules. "Women are warriors," my Chozo parents would squawk as they trained me for battle, "now go practice your ice beam on the Metroids in the basement." The Galactic Federation hired me as a bounty hunter to eradicate the Mother Brain. I kept my femininity a secret, hidden under the bulk of my Power Suit. While it felt liberating to reveal my true self to the universe after completing that first mission more than twenty-six years ago, there is something else I have been hiding: I am a lesbian.

Why have I kept this a secret for so long? That's hard for me to say. The nature of my work forces me to silence. Working as a mercenary, it's far better to let my arm cannon do the talking. Plus, the ways I've chosen to express myself have tended toward the unorthodox. I wrote a book of poems entitled *Morphing Inside My Varia Suit*, which failed to find a publisher. I would flit between one relationship and another, hopping inside my gunship and speeding off to the next planet before things got too serious. Then the Mother Brain decided to outlaw same-sex marriage on planet SR388. Planets Tallon IV and Aether and my birth planet, K-2L, followed suit. What year are we living in? Earth Year 2012? It's time for the universe to redefine its narrow concept of marriage.

The matter is being taken to the Supreme Council of the Galactic Federation, the highest court in the galaxy, for a decision in a few months. While I'm generally in favor of bold measures, this is the wrong way to approach the issue. I am calling for fellow gay-rights advocates to take an incrementalist approach, beginning with small yet important steps, which I call Morph Laws. This trio of measures will set the stage for equal rights amongst all homosexual species.

Morph Law A:
Create a Distinction Between Religious and Civil Marriage
Religion has shaped the institution of marriage. Some of the more prominent religions say that it must be between a man and a woman. Yet other religions, such as ancient Bryyonian, Luminoth, and Alimbic, believe that individuals should be free to marry those of their own sex, even outside their species. Under our constitution, the Galactic Federation has no interest in preferring one religion to another. One of my Chozo guardians, a wise sage named Gray Voice, said, "Beliefs do not fade away." This is why we must separate civil unions from religious ones, with a future amendment granting union to an asexual creature that divides and wishes to marry its other self.

Morph Law B:
Extend Hospital Visitation Rights to Gay Partners
One of the benefits of civil unions would be hospital access, a human rights policy not in place at many of our galaxies' sickbays. I have never told this story until now, but a female lover and I were on an interplanetary cruise ship when a Metroid that had been hiding above a ceiling fan descended on her head and drained her life energy in a matter of seconds. I rushed her to the infirmary, where nurses and doctors attempted to freeze the Metroid with an ice beam and fired

missiles at it five times. At least that's what they told me. I wasn't allowed to see her. Moments later I was informed she was dead. Can an argument be made against this basic human privilege? I'll never see my partner again—the Metroid guaranteed that, but the hospital was just as guilty.

Morph Law C:
Repeal the Federation Police's "Don't Ask, Don't Tell" Policy

The most recent federal law to address a same-sex issue occurred in Earth Year 1996, when the Galactic Federation (then called the U.S. Government) enacted the Defense of Marriage Act. In a way, this measure was my ticket into the military. I didn't shower in the women's barracks. I spoke little to my fellow officers. I could kill energy-sucking Metroids and secretly remain a lesbian. Now I realize this law is another way for the government to discriminate against people like me. Just for writing this piece, I risk never getting any more mercenary assignments. But there's an old saying in the Federation—if you're trying to kill a Space Pirate, the maximum effective range of an excuse is zero meters. It's time for our leaders to stop making them.

These three laws, passed on a planet-by-planet level, carefully steering clear of the conservative Supreme Council, would lead to victory. Internet logs from before the time when Phazon purchased by North Korea destroyed the Earth reveal that U.S. Earthlings passed state laws to lift the ban on gay marriage. There's hope for our planets. Marriage is for the multiplayer. Man and man, woman and woman, or man and woman. Two beings united by love. Who are we to stop that? I expressed this dynamic best in one of my poems, "United with Myself." I wrote: "I am a woman, yet I am a machine / I am a Zebesian, Chozoian / I am a lesbian."

ABSTINENCE-ONLY DRIVER'S ED

Suzanne Kleid

Thanks for making it out on a rainy Saturday, kids. Slippery out there, huh? Let's get started. We're gonna have some fun today!

Car accidents are a leading cause of death for teenagers. The school board and your elected representatives want to make sure that you and your families are spared from such a tragedy, which is why the money for driver's ed was eliminated from the budget. Whereas last year I was teaching your older siblings how to shift and brake and three-point-turn during a six-week course, it has since been decreed that I actually need just one afternoon to tell you the only piece of safety information I'm permitted by law to share:

> The ONLY one hundred percent effective method for avoiding car accidents is to ABSTAIN from driving until marriage.

Yes, yes, I know you've been bombarded with messages from popular culture about how much fun it would be to get behind the wheel of a red convertible, find an unbroken stretch of country road, and, with the wind in your hair, see what she can do. I know that up until now you had the mistaken belief that getting a driver's license was a cherished milestone of your young, sweet, innocent lives. It isn't. It's a milestone, all right: a milestone indicating terrible pain, degradation, and certain death.

"What about seat belts?" you might be saying to yourself. "Don't seat belts GUARANTEE that I CAN'T POSSIBLY die in a car?" *Bzzzt!* Wrongo. Every single day in this country, seat belts FAIL. In fact, I know of a study that proves—CONCLUSIVELY proves, people—that seat belts will fail seventy-five percent of the time.

Who did the study? Government workers.

Well, okay, East German government workers. At a single bribe- and patronage-ridden Trabant factory in 1967.

Moving on.

Along with unbridled premarital driving, we have a group of people who threaten to undermine everything America stands for, and that is your parents. Parents who seem to think it's a good idea to teach their children how to drive a car, to put their precious gifts from the Almighty into the cold twisted-metal hands of certain destruction. "My mom takes me to the church parking lot and lets me practice three-point turns!" you might say. "We only went five miles an hour!"

Kids, please direct your attention to the poster above the black- board here: FASTER THAN PARKED IS FAST ENOUGH TO KILL.

If Grandpa offers to take you out to the cornfield for stick-shift practice or to an empty suburban street so you can practice your parallel parking, YOU ARE STILL DRIVING, AND DRIVING IS WHAT I'M TELLING YOU NOT TO DO. Got it? One day you're shifting with Gramps, and two weeks later the thrill will have worn off and you'll have to up the ante. You'll have to move on to highway driving. Then, standing up, with your head stick- ing out the sunroof, you cruise through the big city at night. Then you'll be doing donuts. Drag racing. Sideshowing. Ghostriding the whip. Tokyo drifting.

Oh sure, ghostriding the whip LOOKS incredibly cool and badass. But when your parents are in the hospital waiting room try- ing to decide whether or not to donate your corneas to science—

because you're BRAIN-DEAD—maybe THEN you'll regret those parallel-parking lessons, hmm?

Please note the other poster, above the door there: DON'T WANT TO DIE? DON'T TRY TO DRIVE. It's just that simple.

Fear not, kids: there's a time in your life when driving a car will cease to be an evil and disgusting shame-riddled experience. That happens after you're married. My husband got me a Corvette for our anniversary. How sweet is that? And take it from me: NO premarital driving could ever have felt as good as the driving my husband and I do together.

Remember this handy little slogan: "No ring on your finger, no hand on the shifter."

Maybe it made more sense in Australia, sure. But the sentiment still holds!

Now, some of you may wonder if it's okay to drive when you're a legal adult yet still unmarried. Sure, it's "not illegal" to drive when you're eighteen. It's also "not illegal" to drive a car at seventeen, six-teen, or even fifteen, if you are so unlucky as to have some of those horrifically overpermissive parents. But that doesn't make it morally right.

Imagine the beautiful gift you'll give your future spouse if you curb your instincts and ABSTAIN from zipping all over town with any boy who sticks a thumb out at you. Think about THAT one.

And for those of you wondering if it's okay for you to learn to drive because you're gay and can't get legally married, well, don't worry your troubled minds about that, because there's no driving where YOU'RE headed. Everyone in Greenwich Village takes the subway.

This is all very serious, guys. The incidence of car crashes in this town has quintupled just since the beginning of Abstinence-Only Driver's Ed six months ago. QUINTUPLED. Do you know how much that is? Me neither, but it proves you need to do exactly what I say. Class dismissed.

Oh, and hey: whichever one of you owns the gray Taurus, you left your lights on.

A 1980S TEEN SEX COMEDY BECOMES POLITICALLY UNCOMFORTABLE

Andrew Golden

{JOHNNY and MACK sit in Johnny's bedroom in front of an Apple IIc with a green screen. Pictures of 1980s models wearing leotards line the walls.}

JOHNNY: You're the computer geek. You figure it out.

MACK: Just a minute, Johnny. (*Typing.*) By my calculations, when we create this woman, she'll have the teeth of Lauren Hutton, the freckles of Cheryl Tiegs, and the acting chops of Christie Brinkley. Then, we'll both lose our virginity!

JOHNNY: Take it easy, nerdenheimer. Just make with the lady.

MACK: Okay, I just need to press this Closed-Apple key, and . . .

{Smoke and fog fill the air. When it clears, a beautiful WOMAN stands in the middle of the room. She is wearing a leotard.}

JOHNNY: All right!

WOMAN: HELLO. I AM HERE TO PLEASE.

JOHNNY: Fix her voice, Mack! She sounds like a robot.

MACK: Okey-dokey, let me just press the Control key . . .

WOMAN: Hello, boys.

JOHNNY: That's better. Hello, yourself. Are you ready to party?

WOMAN: We'll get to that. Let me ask you a question first. What are your feelings on foreign policy?

MACK: Wha—?

WOMAN: Personally, I've had just about enough of the stale whines of pussy McGovernites and their vague, soy-eating peacenikism.

MACK: I'm sorry?

WOMAN: Listen, we're living in a new age, and a new paradigm is necessary. We must maintain American power against foe or so-called friend and not back out of preemptive self-defense because of wimpy Vietnam Syndrome horseshit.

MACK: "Preemptive self-defense" is an oxymoron!

WOMAN: Oh, I see, American freedom is an "oxymoron"? You damn liberals.

MACK: Hey, that's not what I said!

WOMAN: Ohhhh, so that's how it is! There's never any moral clarity when it comes to you limp-wristed bleeding hearts. You sound just like Fidel. And Hitler!

MACK: That's slander!

WOMAN: You're slander. Next thing you know, you'll be telling me carbon emissions are a problem.

MACK: They are a problem!

WOMAN: Well, well, look who worships at the altar of wishy-washy moonbat science! I've got an idea: why don't we just call off American industry altogether! Can I also sell you the Brooklyn Bridge, Mr. Farrakhan?

JOHNNY: You ready to party, baby?

WOMAN: First you have to agree that the protection of American hegemony should recognize no so-called "international law" constraints. Sweden keeps ranking number one on the UN's Human Development Index? Hey, I hear they eat a lot of fish in Sweden. Maybe they'd like a fish made outta cluster-bomb nukes. And do you know who's a member of the UN? That's right, the Soviet Union! I know you must agree with me, Johnny.

MACK: Don't do it, Johnny! I must have accidentally programmed her incorrectly. My computer indicates the Fred Barnes factor is at radioactive levels. Don't sell out!

WOMAN: Ohhh, I see. So conservatives are programmed, eh? But not you, huh? Oh, perish the thought!

MACK: You were programmed! I did it myself!

WOMAN: (*Sarcastically.*) Of course! Let me submit to your will, comrade! You want America to be destroyed, don't you?

MACK: No!!

WOMAN: That wasn't a no.

MACK: Yes, it was!

WOMAN: Well, it wasn't definitive enough. And you just said yes, anyway.

MACK: You're taking me out of context! I said, "Yes, it was" to the "no"!

WOMAN: How's that for muddled logic? "Uh, yes, no, yes, no, death to America, Hezbollah is misunderstood, blah blah blah."

MACK: That's a misrepresentation!

WOMAN: I'm done talking to you. Now, Johnny, your friend Mack here is clearly both anti-American and insane. Do you think the insane should be allowed to run this country?

MACK: How dare you! You're assassinating my character!

WOMAN: Assassination, eh? My goodness, you sound exactly like Sirhan Sirhan. Why are you so angry? What's with this hate and hostility? I think you must have a mental disorder.

MACK: This isn't a fair debating style.

WOMAN: Crybaby. If it weren't for you, we would have won Vietnam. Quagmire, my ass. You think I like being a veteran of our only lost foreign war? Defeated by traitors on college campuses and not by Charlie in the jungle, I'll tell you that much.

MACK: I wasn't even born. And I created you five minutes ago! You couldn't be a veteran.

WOMAN: That's not what this National Guard payment slip says!

JOHNNY: What do I have to do to get into your pants, baby?

WOMAN: You can start by repealing the death tax. If you gut the EPA, run a Southern strategy, and throw a Ronald Reagan film marathon on your dad's Betamax, I may even let you get to third base.

JOHNNY: Meh, *Bedtime for Bonzo*'s probably gonna be a deal-breaker.

FOR A YELLOW BRICK WALL

Mike Gallagher

TO: Editor@TheEmeraldCityTribune.oz
SUBJECT: Illegal Immigration in the Land of Oz!
FROM: J. Spalding Fleabane

Sir,

As Regional Commander of the Minute Men of Munchkinland, I must take issue with the many accusations leveled against my organization by your newspaper.

We are not the xenophobic "gun-toting hobbits" that our detractors have made us out to be. We are loyal patriots. Patriots that are desperately trying to protect the Land of Oz from the rising tide of undocumented American immigrants that is flooding through our highly porous and virtually unguarded borders.

Securing our rainbow frontier is a dangerous, never-ending job. And even though we are dedicated, our diminutive stature prevents us from covering as much ground as we would ultimately like to. On top of that, pesticides, badgers, and freeway crossings are conspiring to thin our ranks daily. And yet we press on, manning our posts atop the scary-high ramparts of Munchkin sovereignty.

Gun control still remains a challenge. Literally. The unfortunate fact is our tiny hands simply weren't designed to handle the tremendous recoil that comes with discharging today's high-powered assault weapons. And sadly, firearms accidents are occurring at an alarming rate—RIP, Captain Tinky Winky Goldenrod, a gallant patriot and a real mensch.

Furthermore, I would also like to state for the record that we are not racists. We have nothing against the American people. For the most part they are a colorful, hardworking lot, and if a DOCUMENTED, law-abiding American wants to work in our candy cane fields or in our sweetshops, I say fine. Just as long as they agree to return to the patch of dust that is their hereditary homeland when the job is over. Frankly, we don't think that's too much to ask.

The trouble arises when certain migrants take advantage of our hospitality. I want to tell you a story about Sally, a spry 163-year-old who wanted nothing more than to spend her golden years growing nightshade and spoiling her cats at her beloved Munchkin Country retreat. Sally was a retired alchemist. I say *was* because on August 29 she was crushed into bonemeal when a flying house landed on her graying crown. Police reports confirm that the errant three-bedroom/one-bath rancher was flown by (you guessed it) an illegal immigrant. What's more, the fourteen-year-old offender didn't even have a real-estate license, much less a pilot's license. And insurance? Oh, please. Her only pitiful explanation was that she was seeking "asylum for her dog." HER DOG!

But it gets worse.

After the American teenager violated Oz airspace (and made carpaccio of a beloved double-octogenarian), she pilfered the decedent's shoes and fled the scene on foot. Unfortunately, the local constabulary didn't have the wherewithal or upper-body strength to administer the blood-alcohol test, but we can pretty much assume what the results of that would have been.

Is this what passes for "senior care" these days?

Wake up, people of Oz, we have a crisis on our hands! And I, for one, do not want to live under skies darkened by wave upon wave of airborne American real estate. After all, one can't help but wonder what the next ungodly edifice to drift over our rainbow border might be. A flying tenement? Or maybe an entire squadron of IHOPs? The whole thing makes me sick to my tummy.

What happens when hulking American factories, teeming with workers, start landing on our enchanted forests? (My God, I can hear the squirrels screaming in mortal terror now.) Will you sit back and let these minimum-wagers take jobs away from our countrymen?

Even now I have heard of migrant activists—some say socialists—who are inciting scarecrows and metallic lumbermen to walk off their jobs in a demand for paychecks and internal organs. This type of slowdown could have an enormous impact on agribusiness down the road. After all, the apple trees aren't going to pick themselves. Okay, maybe they will, but you get my point nonetheless.

I happen to know that other community leaders share our same concerns. In fact, I've reached out to both the Lollypop Guild and the Federated Moonbeam Fitters (Local 86), and they are prepared to use their considerable clout to elect politicians who truly appreciate the gravity of the situation.

So, with all that in mind, I propose what I modestly call "The Fleabane Immigration Initiative." It is a comprehensive action plan predicated on four strategic elements:

1. Mandatory repatriation
2. An extensive yellow brick wall
3. Surface-to-air missiles
4. Flying monkey patrols (or, at the very least, missile-wielding flying monkeys)

But I can't do it alone. I need help. Write the Wizard and urge him to implement my Fleabane Initiative immediately; it's the only way we can prevent Oz from being overrun by long-legged interlopers. Or, better yet, join our happy few. We Minute Men may have a small constituency, but we make up for it with the audacity of our beliefs.

Don't tread on us!

Yours Truly,
J. Spalding Fleabane,
Regional Commander / Spiritual Leader,
Minute Men of Munchkinland

THE STABILITY OF DATA

Ben Greenman

CHANCE THIS CHART WILL CHANGE SLIGHTLY
WHEN YOU LOOK AWAY FROM IT

CHANCE IT WILL NOT

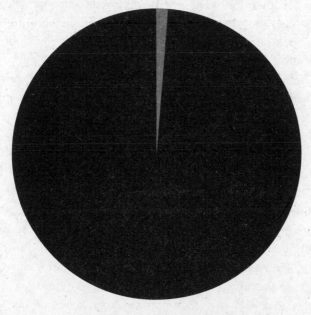

HOW BERNANKE TACKLED THE DEPRESSION, AS RECORDED 150 YEARS FROM NOW BY POST-APOCALYPTIC HOBO FOLKLORISTS

Grant Munroe

Once the great Recession was the scourge of the land. Millions of workers lost their jobs. Those still employed looked out their office windows and saw the jobless in wrinkled suits, stumbling around outside, bumping into one another, moaning in desperation. Some held résumé folders under their arms. It was truly a frightening sight, and those looking on from the office windows were terrified.

When all the great CEOs saw that their employees were terrified, they grew terrified, too.

Terrified employees aren't efficient employees, they fretted.

So the great CEOs banded as one and on hand and knee crawled into their respective corporate jets to make pilgrimage to Capitol Hill. They crawled out of their jets and crawled into their respective black limousines, and out again they crawled all the way up the steps of the Capitol to the meeting of the Senate. There they prostrated themselves before the otherworldly wisdom and power of the great sages of Ways and Means: all were supine, with arms outstretched and faces to the dust.

O you great men, the CEOs intoned, *come to our aid, for Recession stalks the land, necessitating the unfortunate downsizing of underperforming companies, and many are unemployed, and many more are afeard of unemployment, which is just as harsh a kick to the pants, efficiency-wise.*

What, the chorus of sages boomed, *would you have us do, you besuited CEOs?*

You sages, who are closer to the almighty Fed, must ask it to slay this Recession, they wailed. *Or at least palliate its effects by affording us an infusion of capital.*

Thereby it came that the sages conferred amongst themselves for many days in a closed-door session of Congress, and throughout this time called upon the Fed, and its ruler, Bernanke.

O Bernanke, the sages cried, *what sacrifices must we and the great CEOs make unto you, so that you will champion our cause and smite this Recession?*

Bernanke thundered from his throne atop the Fed building:

Three are the sacrifices I demand, and three shall I receive!

First, thou must convince the CEOs to curb executive pay. Second, thou must invite my apostles to more Capitol Hill parties, consenting not to snub them because they are humorless economists by vocation. Finally, you must slaughter for me a hundred oxen of pure white hide.

Thus spake Bernanke.

And so the sages did as Bernanke said. The oxen were slaughtered, and economists were invited to Capitol Hill parties. And lo, they had a conference call with the great CEOs and asked them to cool it with the multimillion-dollar bonus pay, and salaries hundreds of times larger than the lowliest employee under them, and profligate executive retreats on the company's dime. And the CEOs rubbed their noses and scratched their chins and looked elsewhere before finally murmuring a promise that they would look into it.

The three sacrifices thus made, Bernanke set loose 999 economists, each of whom met with 999 government officials, each of whom drafted 999 new policy initiatives, each new initiative being but one component in a tremendous spell, one thread woven with all the others to make a maddeningly complex hex, one that slowly, very slowly, transformed Bernanke from mere mortal to a ten-thousand-foot colossus. It was then that the Speaker of the House armed him with the Capitol dome as a shield, and the Secretary of the Treasury armed him with the Empire State Building as a sword.

Bernanke roared in celebration of his might, and his roar was heard all around the world, sending both anarcho-capitalists and neo-utopian socialists trembling together, as if brothers.

So it happened that Bernanke then stalked the Rust Belt, the favorite and longtime haunt of the Recession, before spying in the distance a much greater foe than expected: not Recession—but Depression ascendant. The Scourge of Markets sat glumly, sipping coffee from a nuclear cooling tower just outside of Bridgman, Michigan. He was listening to the wails of the unemployed, which to him sounded as pleasing and melancholy as any Coldplay album. Knowing the strength of his enemy was too great to confront on the level field of battle, Bernanke, being a wise and crafty man, disguised himself.

Hey there, greeted Bernanke.

Oh, hey, said Depression with disinterest. He started absently clipping his toenails with the hinged trunk of an unsold 2009 Chevy Impala.

I'm just a stupid Natural Resources Boom, said Bernanke, *and so I'm a bit lost. Is this the way to the Alberta Oil Sands?*

Depression coughed. He wiped his nose, then lit a cigarette made from an automotive factory smokestack and ten thousand pounds of grade-C soy by-product. He jabbed behind him, over his shoulder. *Yeah, it's over there,* he said. *You should probably go through Ontario.*

Bernanke asked if Depression wouldn't mind showing him the way. Depression sighed.

Fine, he said, with eye-rolling exasperation. *But watch your step. I took a dump somewhere just outside Windsor.*

So Depression led the way.

And lo, it was then, just as Depression was about to step over the Detroit River, that Bernanke hit him across the head with the Empire State Building.

Son of a gun! cried Depression, clutching his ear.

Before Depression knew what was happening, Bernanke tackled him into Lake Erie, where the two thrashed about for days and days, with the tenacity of two drunks in a gutter fight. Finally, Bernanke won the upper hand. He smashed Depression's head five times against Toledo and dunked his head five times under the Maumee River. Depression cried uncle.

Okay, I give up. What do you want?

By my steel-wool beard, boomed Bernanke, *I command you to leave this land at once!*

Ah man, I was just getting comfortable here, Depression whined.

Eager to have Depression vacate the premises without a further, prolonged fight, Bernanke used $999 billion in bailout money to pay back Depression's security deposit. Depression tucked the check into his shirt pocket. That's when Bernanke chucked Depression far, far away—all the way to the middle of the Atlantic Ocean, where Depression sank, pouting, waiting morosely for the next business cycle that would carry him ashore.

The whole nation exploded in celebration. The unemployed became employed. The employed regained their efficiency. The CEOs lavished the sages of Capitol Hill with gifts of gold and fine linens and campaign contributions. And Bernanke returned home to the Fed a hero to all. But in short time he grew smaller as the policies grew more and more outmoded, until he shrank to human size, retired from office, and joined the lecture circuit—soon to be forgotten by everyone save for his loyal disciples, the economists, who bided time just as morosely as Depression.

Time they had, these economists—and in excess—until, of course, 2012.

RON PAUL GIVES A GUIDED TOUR OF
HIS NAVAJO ART COLLECTION

Jeremiah Tucker

We'll begin with one of my favorite pieces. This is a rare early-twentieth-century photogravure of a Navajo sandpainting, drawn by an unnamed medicine man for a four-day ritual called the Red Antway ceremony. Now, a lot of people—even in Congress—simply don't understand how traditional Navajo customs work. The Navajo believe ants are messengers from the Red Ant People who live in the holy lands below the earth, and the sandpainting acts as a conduit through which the ant people cure a child of any illness.

Pictorial representations of authentic Navajo sandpaintings—sometimes called drypaintings—are incredibly rare because, according to custom, the medicine man typically destroys the art within hours of its creation, and outsiders are rarely allowed into the ceremonies. Years ago I was lucky enough to learn how to draw many traditional sandpaintings from a Navajo medicine man, but as a *bilagáana*, I never used the healing ceremonies in my medical practice. (*Laughs.*) Except once at the parents' request. The boy died a horrible death.

The tour will pause now while I sing a song from the Kinaaldá ceremony, which celebrates the first menstrual cycle of a young woman. (*Sings for half an hour.*)

Thank you, thank you. But I know it's the beautiful song you're applauding and not these dusty old pipes.

(*Laughs. Takes off his shoes and slips on a pair of moccasins.*)

I don't often talk about this, but I draw a lot of inspiration from the Navajo people's traditional way of life. Growing up, whenever my friends and I would play cowboys and Indians, I was always the American Indian. Up here, sometimes I still am. Now, maybe I'm romanticizing something that could never have existed the way I picture it, but in my head, it's pretty great.

(*Wraps himself in a Navajo rug.*)

This piece is neat, huh? It's a nineteenth-century chief's blanket made from Navajo-Churro wool. Notice the traditional bars and simple color scheme that mark this as a first-phase design. It was actually the Spanish who introduced sheep to what would later become known as the American Southwest, but the Navajo proved to be expert shepherds. And soon sheep became so vital to Navajo culture that wool almost completely supplanted cotton in their weaving, a gift given to the Navajo by the holy person Spider Woman.

Interesting fact: early in my political career I actually introduced a bill in Congress that would've abolished our current system of fractional-reserve banking and made sheep our national currency. Had it passed, you could've walked into your local Walmart and paid for your purchases with a sack of wool that, unlike our paper money, possesses a legitimate value in the marketplace. Unfortunately, the bill sunk because we could never figure out what one would use to pay for the sheep themselves. Negotiations broke down over the cost of a grilled rack of lamb, which I thought would be roughly equivalent to a merino wool sweater, but Southern Democrats disagreed vehemently.

(*Picks up a pair of turquoise earrings and puts them on.*)

Of course, I've since advocated returning to a national currency of silver and gold. Did you know the Navajo are skilled silversmiths? There is some disagreement about when the Navajo began making the silver jewelry they're so well known for among today's more discerning tourists, but I personally believe it began around 1850. For centuries earlier, however, the Navajo made jewelry from turquoise, a semiprecious blue stone that also wouldn't make a bad national currency.

(*Removes shirt and slides a patterned silver bracelet up his arm. Wraps a different Navajo rug known as an "eyedazzler" around his shoulders.*)

Today it's illegal for anyone to advertise something as Native American art if it wasn't, in fact, made by a Native American. Hogwash! Sure, the absence of such a law puts a little more responsibility on the buyer, but if you can't tell an 1863 Navajo belt concho from an 1863 Mexican belt concho, then you shouldn't be in the market for period-specific belt conchos. Mercy!

(*Drops pants, shimmies into buckskin breechcloth.*)

You know, when I'm up here among my Navajo arts and stuff, I have a hard time pinpointing when America lost its way. Was it with LBJ's Great Society? Roosevelt's New Deal? The year 1913, when we were saddled with the income tax and the IRS? Abraham Lincoln squashing states' rights? Maybe it was the Anti-Federalists caving to the Federalists and agreeing to pass the Constitution?

Well, I think it goes back further. Before there was an America, America started going down the tubes. The Navajo and Native Indians had it right from the get-go. I think inside each of us is a noble Navajo warrior yearning to ride forth from his log-and-mud hogan toward the Black Mesa with Father Sky above, Mother Earth below, and worthy enemies all around—as unbridled as the horsey beneath him.

(*Begins whipping around a traditional Navajo bullroarer.*)

TRIBAL MATTERS

Jim Stallard

Congressional Record
Monday, November 7, 2011
House of Representatives
The SPEAKER: This morning's proceedings will be devoted to discussion of H.R. 416, the Demetrification Act of 2011. I will be offering my own comments in support of this legislation, which forbids use of the metric system in our federally funded laboratories. But first, we have a brief resolution to dispense with. The Chair recognizes the gentleman from Virginia (Mr. SCOTT) for five minutes.

Mr. SCOTT: Mr. Speaker, I rise today to note that exactly 200 years ago, on November 7, 1811, the Battle of Tippecanoe was won through the courageous leadership of William Henry Harrison, who was born in my district. For those of us who've forgotten our high-school history, the Battle of Tippecanoe is considered by many to be the opening battle of the War of 1812. More important, the battle meant the defeat of Tenskwatawa, who with his brother Tecumseh had formed a confederation of numerous tribes to block American expansion to the west. Tippecanoe was the turning point for driving out the Indians so our forefathers could fulfill this country's Manifest Destiny. On behalf of all Americans, I honor William Henry Harrison for allowing this nation to achieve the greatness ordained for it in the eyes of God. Thank you.

The SPEAKER: I'm sure we have bipartisan agreement on that—if nothing else—today. (*Laughter in the chamber.*) Now down to the business at hand. The Chair recognizes the gentleman from South Carolina (Mr. MULVANEY) for five minutes.

Mr. MULVANEY: Mr. Speaker, with all respect to my Virginia colleague, I feel it necessary to note that Andrew Jackson from my district was the real driving force behind Indian removal. Before his heroic efforts, many of our southern states were teeming with savages. As President, he oversaw the relocation of 45,000 Indians to the west so our ancestors could lay claim to their birthright. Elites in Washington like John Marshall tried to tell Old Hickory that these squatters had rights just like Americans, but Jackson knew what had to be done. Let's not have any more of this revisionist history. Andrew Jackson rooted out this country's original Red Menace, and we should never forget it. Thank you.

Mr. GIBSON: (*Leaping to his feet*) Mr. Speaker, this is an outrage. It is—

The SPEAKER: You are speaking out of turn. You must be recognized before taking the floor.

Mr. GIBSON: I'm not waiting for anything. I won't sit here and listen to perverse accounts of how this country was cleansed. It is well established that although the Indian Removal Act was passed under President Jackson, it was Martin Van Buren who sent in the armed forces and annihilated their way of life. Mr. Jackson seemed to think that the best way to deal with Indians was to pal around with them and sign treaties. Martin Van Buren knew that you do not negotiate with savages. You burn their homes, destroy and plunder their property, and execute tribal leaders. If you want to know why our children aren't being served pemmican for school lunch, you can thank Martin Van Buren. He converted the Trail of Tears from a dream into reality.

The SPEAKER: Gentlemen, we cannot continue with these breaches of protocol. Apart from that, we're here to discuss H.R. 416. Now . . . The Chair recognizes the gentleman from Pennsylvania (Mr. MURPHY) for five minutes.

Mr. MURPHY: Appalling. I'm sitting here and I can't believe my ears. My colleagues should be ashamed of themselves. To turn their backs on one of this nation's most heroic acts . . . Let me remind you of two words that used to mean something to Americans: *Smallpox. Blankets.* This nation's divine fate was sealed when William Trent bestowed the disease-ridden cloth upon our enemy during the siege of Fort Pitt. Among historians, there is no dispute that infectious diseases from Europe killed the most Indians. Everything else is the stuff of Hollywood movies. I'm aware that success has many fathers, as the saying goes, but it's disgusting to sit here today and listen to people in this chamber usurp the work of William Trent—and of God—for their own constituents.

The SPEAKER: Gentlemen, I ask you once more to—

Mr. MULVANEY: I'll take five more minutes, Mr. Speaker. First, that ridiculous smallpox-and-blankets myth was discredited by historians long ago. I don't know where Mr. MURPHY gets his information, but William Trent killed exactly zero Indians using that method, and probably any other method. Second, Andrew Jackson may have signed treaties with various tribes, but it's not like he *honored* any of them. I will not have his good name besmirched by Mr. Gibson. Andrew Jackson had plenty of Indian blood on his calloused, populist hands. Martin Van Buren? (*Falsetto*) Oooh, let's send in the troops to deal with the scary people! I don't want to get near them. Besides, it's time for my manicure.

Mr. GIBSON: (*Angrily*) Really? (*Falsetto*) Oooh, I'm Andrew Jackson. Here's the deed to my country, Running Bear. Let's sit down and have tea. I sure hope they build a Native American museum someday on the National Mall.

Mr. MURPHY: Hi, everyone! I'm two insecure representatives ignoring well-established epidemiologic history.

The SPEAKER: Enough! (*Very emotional*) You know . . . People kid me all the time about how easily I cry. But this kind of thing just tears me up inside. Displacement of the Indians is a legacy we all share. It doesn't belong to this or that hero. It's woven into the fabric of our nation. Can't we accept that and move forward?

Mr. SCOTT: Mr. Speaker, in the interest of comity, I would like to withdraw my resolution.

The SPEAKER: (*Visibly moved*) Thank you, Mr. SCOTT.

Mr. SCOTT: But I want a provision in H.R. 416 that William Henry Harrison be thanked at the end of every research grant proposal.

The SPEAKER: Goddamn all of you. Get another babysitter. I'll be at Apache Casino.

EARLY DRAFTS OF PATRICK HENRY'S REVOLUTIONARY PROCLAMATION "GIVE ME LIBERTY OR GIVE ME DEATH!"

Sam Weiner

"Give me liberty or give me death! Or give me both! Preferably liberty first and then death several decades after that and even then in an easy, comfortable way if it has to happen at all!"

"Give me liberty or give me death! Or give me a mix of both, where I get a little bit of liberty for a few hours each day but then somebody comes and pinches me on the arms once a week."

"Give me liberty AND give me death! But only give me death to all the people who hate liberty and give me liberty to all the people who hate liberty to death!"

"Give me liberty or give me a spicy, tomato-based hot sauce flavored with chilies, onion, garlic, and cilantro! You could dip corn chips in it!"

"Give me liberty and check out this cool national seal I designed— one side has an eagle holding a bunch of arrows in its claws and the other side has a pyramid with an eyeball floating on top of it! It came to me in a dream!"

"Give me liberty or give me—hold up. Do you guys realize how much tail we're gonna get if this revolution goes well?"

"Give me liberty or give me a nation run by tyrannical spider-people with robot arms and acid-breath and they leave cobwebs everywhere and make everyone work in hot caves all day and nobody wants that, so our only viable option out of those two is liberty!"

"Give me liberty or give me unlimited corporate expenditures to influence elections—I'm just kidding! Like the rest of the Founding Fathers, I consider that a form of liberty!"

UNPUBLISHED FEDERALIST PAPERS

Maggie Ryan Sandford

"Methods of Affecting French Vernacular to Promote an Atmosphere of Sophistication Within the Proposed Union"

"The Alleged Tendency to Avoid Discussing the Utility of Slave Labor Considered"

"The Influence of Lady Parts"

"The Insufficiency of the Present Confederation When Defraying Their Alehouse Debts This Fortnight Past"

"The Real Character of the Christian in Government Especially in Regards to Indian Phantasms and Armament Specific to Their Hocus-Pocus"

"These Departments Should Not Be So Far Separated as to Sacrifice the Ability to Whisper Sarcasms Amongst Themselves"

"The Executory Branch"

"Advantage of the Possession of a Lancaster Rifle in Representing an Enviable Manhood Especially in Comparison to the Greatcoat Pistol, Which is Commonly Known to Be Exclusive to Macaronies"

"The Appointing Power Continued and the Power of the Executive Regarding the Democratic Power to Power with Powers in Power"

"The Martial Milieu"

"Certain General and Miscellaneous Objections to the Constitution Briefly Considered and Dismissed Outright"

CRATE & BARREL TABLEWARE STYLE + U.S. PRESIDENT = FICTIONAL DELTA BLUES SINGER

Josh Michtom

Bumble Bee Washington
Normandy Blue Adams
Faded Rose Jefferson
Loop Madison
Domo Pearl Monroe
Roulette Blue Band Adams
Blooms and Buds Jackson
Studio Blue Van Buren
Fish Plate Harrison
Blue Footed Tyler
Boscoware Polk
Oak Leaf Taylor
Nickel Footed Fillmore
Chowder Bowl Pierce
Davenport Buchanan
Wheatstraw Lincoln

PATRIOTIC LAUNDRY METAPHORS

Doogie Horner

These colors don't run.

Even if these colors are in hot water, they will not shrink from their duty.

These colors don't run, but they do bleed—and they're willing to, if need be.

These colors don't like to be hung out to dry.

These colors don't need to be washed in the gentle cycle, because they are tough.

These colors don't like change because it rattles around in the dryer.

These colors are dyed in the wool, the wool of American eagles and our wooly forefathers.

Separate these colors from darker colors, especially if they've entered the laundry illegally and now want these colors to pay for their detergent.

Colors may bleed red, white, and blue.

These colors can handle tough stains like grass and the blood of innocent civilians.

Before putting these colors in the laundry, remember to consult washing instructions on the Constitution.

These colors have the right to life, liberty, and the pursuit of snappy dress.

These colors can iron out any wrinkles in the fabric of America by using hot steel and a can-do attitude.

These colors will always stick together, especially if you don't use an anti-static cling dryer sheet.

These colors go great with any outfit.

These colors don't change. You're thinking of Hypercolor.

These colors are red with anger, blue in the face, and white with you, Uncle Sam!

Freedom isn't wrinkle-free.

QUIZ: RUMSFELD MEMOIR CHAPTER TITLE OR GERMAN HEAVY METAL SONG?

David Rees

Known and Unknown, Donald Rumsfeld's bestselling memoir, features the former Defense Secretary's "unique and often surprising observations on eight decades of history." It was published in February 2011.

War from a Harlots Mouth (WFAHM), a German heavy metal band, features a musical style "combining tech metal, grindcore, hardcore, and jazzy influences." It was founded in 2005.

For this quiz, you must decide whether the following titles are chapters in *Known and Unknown* or WFAHM songs.

You will have **fifteen seconds** to complete this quiz.

1. "Smiling Death"

2. "What Happens in the District . . . "

3. "Crooks at Your Door"

4. "The Dead Enders"

5. "The Job That Couldn't Be Done"

6. "How to Disconnect from Your Social Surroundings in Half an Hour"

7. "Hands Off the Bicycle Seat"

8. "Bears in the Woods"

9. "Briefing Security Werewolves on Red Alert"

10. "The District Attorneys Are Selling Your Blood"

11. "The Polyglutamine Pact"

12. "And in the Right to Make Mistakes, We May Lose Everything and Start Again"

13. "Into the Swamp"

14. "A Grotesque Relationship"

15. "The End-Time Message Part I"

16. "Fighting Wars with Keyboards"

17. "An Agonizing Reappraisal"

18. "The Agony of Surprise"

19. "The Increased Sensation of Dullness"

20. "Gardening"

ANSWER KEY: (1) chapter, (2) song, (3) song, (4) chapter, (5) chapter, (6) song, (7) chapter, (8) chapter, (9) song, (10) song, (11) song, (12) song, (13) chapter, (14) song, (15) song, (16) song, (17) chapter, (18) chapter, (19) song, (20) chapter.

THE NEXT WAVE: CANDIDATE PRODUCT PLACEMENT

Pete Reynolds

Citizens of Iowa, fellow Americans, eighteen- to thirty-four-year-old consumers: Thank you for the opportunity to speak with you here today.

As you know, America is facing challenges. Challenges to our economic stability. Challenges to our way of life. Pepsi Challenges.

As I travel across this great land, I see too many Americans stung by the poor decisions of leaders who can't stop racking up debt—debt that our children and grandchildren will have to answer for. We must stop our addiction to spending, particularly when our spending does not go on a Chase Freedom® Visa card, which offers two percent cash back on purchases, including gas and groceries, as well as points toward flights on most major airlines.

I recently met a woman in Ohio named Carol Time Warner. Mrs. Time Warner was laid off by the local auto-parts factory after sixteen years of dedicated service. After noting the extensive coverage and reasonable costs of UnitedHealthcare's individual plans, she told me she had sent her résumé to over eighteen hundred employers— good, solid, backbone-of-the-American-Dream employers like Pfizer, Applebee's, and The Home Depot, each of which sent her a bouquet of lilies and a handwritten reply expressing a desire to hire her just

as soon as they could get out from under the heavy tax burden sup-
ported by people like my opponent—and yet she still could not find
a job.

Should Mrs. Time Warner be tossed aside? Should she be stuffed
into a Glad Kitchen ForceFlex® Odorshield® trash bag, made with
Stretchable Strength® technology to prevent rips, and taken out to
the curb, to be discarded along with all of your toughest household
messes? I say no. Americans are tired of broken promises and failed
policies. Americans are tired of not having a voice. Well, I'm here to
tell you: I hear your voice. I also watch *The Voice*, Mondays at 8 / 7
central on NBC.

At this time, I'd like to pause and remind all of you of the enor-
mity of what's at stake here today: nothing less than our economic
future, our national security, and, of course, a brand-new 2012 Kia
Sorento®. So, for each of you who purchased a raffle ticket, go ahead
and check it for the winning number: 00429118. Present the winning ticket to any of my campaign staff members wearing a yellow
jacket, and they'll get you on your way. The 2012 Sorento®: A departure from the expected.

Make no mistake: these are critical times, and this is a critical election. We cannot wait any longer for Washington to realize that it has a leadership vacuum. And that vacuum is powerful.
And I should clarify here that I am not even referring to partisan
gridlock, or unaccountable politicians. I am quite literally talking
about a vacuum— the Leadership Vacuum®, the latest innovation
from Dyson®. Goodbye, inefficient bags. Hello, Dual Cyclone™
technology.

That's Dyson®, folks.

God bless you, and God bless America®.

OCCUPY MAIN STREET!

Teddy Wayne

Brothers and brothers! (There are no sisters here, right? Okay, good.) Thank you all for bravely taking your helicopters out to the suburbs tonight to this so-called "Applebee's" dining establishment to stage a sit-in on imported French divans. We will make our voices heard, whether it's from chanting by our assistants, Tweeting via our assistants' assistants' intelligent phones, or getting exposure through the national media outlets we own.

For far too long we have been under the thumb of politicians elected by the masses. The government may throw us a bone with the Electoral College, a small group of elites who officially choose the president, but they always cave in to the popular vote. This spineless democratic pandering is not the kind of leadership deserving of our loophole-reduced four percent federal income tax. We need honorable men with polysyllabic names that sound British, culled from the top boarding schools and Ivy League secret societies, who will dictate policy according to the guidelines proposed in our clandestine meetings and jotted down by our third-level assistants! This is America!

Our demands are as simple as the plebeian wine-drinker's palate. Stricter regulation of corporate-employee finances, such as those of out-of-control Duluth bank clerk Joseph Plummer! Yes to more of those blue shirts with the white collars that Michael Douglas wore in *Wall Street*! No to costly wars that don't involve the control of oil, but if they do, then let's definitely think about it, or, even better, act quickly, then later let others ineffectually think about it because we've already gone in, and now it's too late to get out!

This country was founded on the proposition that all landowning white men with wigs are created equal. Somehow we've gotten away from that mission, and now bewigged men are ridiculed and considered lesser. We are working with the Wigmakers of America to overturn that prejudice. If you can't donate stock options to the cause, we will gladly take hair. Every follicle helps.

Ah, looks like our food reserves have arrived from the outside: soda bottles filled with Dom Pérignon Rosé Vintage 1959 and pizza-flavored foie gras. Mmm—who wants a little fresh-sprayed pepper?

Lock arms in solidarity, after first putting on your suit-sleeve protectors to prevent abrasions that might degrade fine Italian wool. Someone know a fiery protest song that won't infringe upon any intellectual property rights? And a slogan we can print on T-shirts and sell at a three-hundred-percent markup? And a T-shirt factory in Asia with lax workplace oversight?

Remember, the power is with us; *we* are the one percent. And for those who might forget that important number, we've struck an endorsement deal with Big Milk. Our faces are on their cartons, because we've been "missing" from American politics for literally *weeks*.

Let's line up in an orderly fashion to be replaced overnight by our interns' interns. See you in the morning—not too early, so we can all squeeze in a game of racquetball and a sauna. Maybe tomorrow we can lock out the customers who have so callously crossed our police-enforced picket line. Which one of us here owns Applebee's?

OPERATION MIDDLE CLASS: A FEARFUL RICH MAN'S RULES FOR SURVIVAL IN AN INCREASINGLY POPULIST WORLD

Luke Kelly-Clyne

Thank you for meeting me at this small-town diner, where nothing's made of leather or brass, and waiters are allowed to look you in the eye. Pick up a menu. Yes, with your own two hands. Order a cherry-flavored soda with ice and something inexpensive to eat. Something ricey or fried or something. No, not couscous! Are you trying to get us killed?! Something with cheese and sour cream. Something that says, "I make under eight million dollars a year."

Okay, listen. I have to ask you something very important. Do I seem middle class to you? Dammit, take that Patek Philippe off. Someone might see! Do I look middle class, I said? With my plaid button-down, iPod shuffle, and boot-cut jeans. I ask because you're my oldest friend. We've known each other since we were kids, since yacht camp, and now that we're here, safe within the confines of this bargain-bin, honey-mustard shrine to plebeian athletic pastimes, I can explain.

The simple truth of it is, we're in danger. Yes, you too. And that camel-hair jacket isn't helping. Neither is the hovercraft you've parked in the handicapped spot outside. You should ask your man to move it. You drove it yourself? What?! This is what I mean.

Can't you see we're being persecuted? Who? All of us. We, men of incredible means. The world has changed. It's no longer safe to be rich. Each day, the stock market slumps farther and farther. Unemployment runs rampant. A revolution is brewing and we can't afford to be on the wrong side of it. Well, of course we can afford it. We can afford everything, but not without a bit of inconvenience, and is that *really* something you can bear? *Inconvenience?* I know I can't.

Why, just last week, Winston was given a ticket while driving his Maserati through a steamfitters' union march. A ticket! Are you hearing me?! He hit *one* steamfitter. And then yesterday, Monty's private jet was delayed from taking off. Even though he said he needed to get to Vail *quickly*. His pilot didn't even explain the wait. I mean, he explained, but not adequately. The list of atrocities goes on. Mallory's son stepped in a puddle and his nanny didn't immediately kneel down to blow on his dampened feet. The poor boy's only twenty-three. George hasn't been delivered a decently packaged truffle in nearly a week. Simone's assistant didn't immediately update Firefox on Simone's dog's iPad. When Simone asked why, the assistant said she had to "use the bathroom."

Now, do you think this would've happened in 2004? When it was safe to be rich, when people still treated us like damned human beings? Of course not. But this isn't 2004. It's 2011, and we need to protect ourselves. We need to fit in. We need to act like regular people. People who don't blow up BMWs on the Fourth of July, people who don't have indoor squash courts or live-in acupuncturists or seashell rooms. It's for our protection, for our families' protection. It won't be easy, but neither was stomaching Ted Turner's chef's toasted raisin brioche at last year's Private Island Raffle. Listen closely to what I say and you'll be safe from the horrors our people have endured. I'd rather be middle class than put out. Wouldn't you?

We must kick off our Ferragamo driving moccasins and relearn to walk in Skechers, or whatever shoes common people wear. We actually have to do more research on that. I'm not even wearing shoes right now. I didn't want to take any chances.

Cars? Two only, my friend. And your garage should be detached.

If you want to live, that is. Stop sipping your soda so daintily. Gulp it. Are you listening to me?

No more prep schools for the kids. Public only. And they'll take a bus. Riding on house servants' backs is strictly forbidden now.

Complain a lot about paying taxes, and remember, you've never heard the words "offshore account."

Be impressed by things made of cashmere and widen your eyes in surprise when you see one-karat diamonds. Forget that you used to flush them down the toilet like daddy longlegs spiders.

Only take pain medications when you're in pain.

When you go skiing, you're going to stay in something called a "condo." Chalets are as dead to you as your Merck board appointment. Which reminds me, resign from Merck's board.

"Water cooler talk" refers to conversations people partake in when procrastinating at their office jobs. It has nothing to do with speculating on plastic futures for your bottled-water conglomerate.

A cleaning lady will come once per week. She will be in too much of a hurry to make you eggs Benedict or rid your private Manhattan "weekend place" of deceased prostitutes. Luckily, you'll no longer have a Manhattan weekend place.

Central Florida is now an unironically appealing vacation destination.

Oh, oh, this is big. *Wish* for things you don't have. Regular people can actually think of things they want that they *don't* already own. No, they *can't* just buy them. That's the whole point! Do you understand? Tell me you understand.

I've imparted everything I know. But I'm learning more every day. Keep your eyes and ears open and you will, too. All I can ask is that you trust me and, please, live below your means. For all of our kind. Now, hand over all the gold you have on you. Wait, shut up. Here comes the waiter. Try to get a look at his shoes.

I WILL

Henry Alford

The next time you hear from me, I'll have some very exciting news. We're just dotting the i's on this one.

I've started a conversation with the American people. It's a conversation we've been meaning to have for a long time.

Yes, everything you've heard is true: I'm cementing my reputation as a leader to be watched.

I can't put it any more plainly: I'm unofficially official.

Starting today, I've got a beady eye on the future. The future is all-important to me, and it's from where I'll draw my strength—my strength to throw my hat into the ring. That's right, folks—I am soon going to tell you that I am going to throw my hat into the ring, and when that hat lands, you will have a powerful new association with all metaphors related to throwing and hats.

The way I see it, it's like this: I've got a mandate with the future, and because that mandate is about the future, that's when I'm going to tell you about it—in the future. Anything I say now would be premature. French president Nicolas Sarkozy called me yesterday and said, "Well, Henry—any news?" And I had to tell him, "Nick, I wouldrai if I couldrai, but right this second I can'trai."

Will. Interesting word, no? It has at least two meanings, and I like to think that I embody them both. And I also like to think that

I have some of that word's amazing resolve. Because, think about it: knock the *w* off the front end of *will* and what are you left with? I'll. *I'll.* It may be true, as John Donne once wrote, that no man is an island, but *this* man is a definite I'll. A very, very definite I'll.

You and I make a good team, Voter. We can make this happen together. And once we've decided what it is, it will only be that much more real to us. We know it's bold. We know it makes us feel better about who we are. We know it makes a better world for our children. But what is it specifically, and why does it answer to the name President?

I'll tell you. Tomorrow.

WORD PROBLEMS FOR FUTURE
HEDGE FUND MANAGERS

Bob Woodiwiss

Elementary
(AGES 5–10)

1. Dick has $1 million. Jane has $1 million. If Dick and Jane both give their $1 million to T. Boone, how many millions will he claim he can turn it into?

2. On his way home from school, Kyle stops to buy a candy bar. It costs 69¢. How much change should Kyle get back if he pays for the candy with a $1,000,000,000 bill?

3. Among those earning ten-figure incomes, Mr. Soros's total annual compensation is greater than Mr. Falcone's. Mr. Falcone's is greater than Mr. Griffin's. Mr. Griffin's is smaller than Mr. Soros's, and Mr. Paulson's is greater than Mr. Soros's. In descending order, list the men by the respective hotness of their wives.

4. A hedge fund manager gets up at 5 a.m. It takes him 12 minutes to shower, 8 minutes to get dressed, and 20 minutes to eat breakfast. How big is his domestic staff?

Intermediate
(AGES 11–15)

1. Your middle-class parents have a combined household income of $115,000. You receive an allowance of $20 per week. If you save all your allowance for two years, how much debt will you have to finance to hostilely take over your family? How will you structure the debt?

2. The number of hours left in the New York Stock Exchange's trading day is one-third of the number of hours already passed. How many hours are there until you can start trading on the Tokyo Stock Exchange?

3. At 10 a.m., a private Gulfstream G650 takes off from New York, headed south to the Caribbean island of St. Barts, traveling at a speed of Mach .9. At 11 a.m., a private Gulfstream G550 takes off from St. Barts, headed north to New York, traveling at Mach .885. Both jets fly at 50,000 feet on parallel flight paths. When the aircraft pass each other somewhere over the Atlantic, how long after seeing the G650 will the owner of the G550 kick himself for not going top-of-the-line? (Answer should be expressed in nautical miles.)

4. In a given year, the Dow Jones Industrial Average rises 8.3 percent, the NASDAQ rises 7.6 percent, and the S&P 500 rises 7.9 percent. If, in that same period, you manage a $29 billion hedge fund that loses 11.6 percent, how large a year-end bonus are you entitled to? (Round to the nearest $10 million.)

Advanced
(AGES 16–18)

1. Mr. Smith is being investigated by the SEC for insider trading. Calculate the probability of Mr. Smith's relocation to Dubai.

2. If an American hedge fund manager makes $900 million and is taxed at a rate of 15 percent, how many American factory workers making $32,500 and being taxed at a rate of 25 percent does that make a sucker of? (Show your work.)

3. Your mother gives you x dollars to put gas in the family car.

Your father gives you y dollars to get a haircut. You lose $x + y$ dollars betting against your high school's undefeated football team. Explain to your familial investors how "that's life."

4. Days before the housing bubble bursts, you short the ABX subprime index and, when the ensuing mortgage crisis causes millions of families to lose their homes to foreclosure, you realize a $550 million profit. Since, for you, this is the opposite of a problem, find the opposite of an answer.

MOM'S AND DAD'S CAMPAIGN STATEMENTS

Gregory Beyer

MOM'S CAMPAIGN SPOKESWOMAN: Mom finds it disappointing, though not surprising, that, since the argument last month, Dad has dyed his hair brown, bought a fancy new car, and taken to wearing Loose Fit blue jeans, proving that he is out of touch with gray-haired, old-car-driving, Classic Fit–wearing Americans. The effort is emblematic of twenty years of failed Dad policies, not to mention a misuse of family funds, providing a glimpse of how Dad would embarrass the whole family, instead of just himself, if forgiven.

DAD'S CAMPAIGN SPOKESMAN: Dad's actions are a direct result of Mom's "Sleeping in Separate Beds" policy, for which he plans to seek reparations when forgiven, and which Mom enacted, in a shameless effort to dredge up past grievances, on September fourth, the twenty-second anniversary of Grandma's historic "But He's Jewish" speech.

MOM'S CAMPAIGN SPOKESWOMAN: It may interest Dad to know that when Mom implemented the "Sleeping in Separate Beds" initiative on September fourth, it was not, as she claimed at the time, because she suffers from restless legs syndrome.

DAD'S CAMPAIGN SPOKESMAN: The revelation that she lied about restless legs syndrome, a debilitating condition affecting millions of Americans and therefore not to be kicked around, is indicative of Mom's long-standing culture of deception—though it's just as well, since Dad has an established record of not really wanting to touch varicose veins. Oh, did Mom really think Dad didn't notice? Dad's noble refusal to utter the words "gross" or "so, so sick" in reference to the veins, or to say during car trips that "we're not there yet, but we're getting varicose," reflects the tone of civility that has been the hallmark of Dad since his life began, about three months after his conception. And Mom's lies are all the more startling in light of the fact that Dad is an American hero.

MOM'S CAMPAIGN SPOKESWOMAN: Mom has repeatedly expressed her utmost respect and gratitude to Dad for the two hours he spent locked in the second-floor bathroom at the 2003 Stevenson dinner party.

DAD'S CAMPAIGN SPOKESMAN: Dad's two hours and twelve minutes in the bathroom, during which Mom indulged in the carefree, selfish practice of feeding herself, exposed the faulty lock installed on the Stevenson bathroom door and directly led to its replacement. At a subsequent holiday party in 2007, Dad returned to the second-floor bathroom, in spite of the lingering trauma and Carol Stevenson's announcement that the first-floor powder room, which was much closer, had just been redone.

MOM'S CAMPAIGN SPOKESWOMAN: Mom has repeatedly acknowledged Dad's courage in returning to the bathroom and has the utmost respect for him and other Americans who, because of faulty locks or their own gross incompetence, get locked in.

DAD'S CAMPAIGN SPOKESMAN: Mom's acknowledgment of Dad's heroism rings hollow, since Mom joked to Carol Stevenson after the party that Dad was not actually locked in the bathroom but seeking refuge because he hated having to hear Don and Cindy Blake brag about their son Ronald and the Princeton rowing team.

MOM'S CAMPAIGN SPOKESWOMAN: Mom has always felt that Don Blake is a tool.

DAD'S CAMPAIGN SPOKESMAN: Mom's characterization of Don Blake as "a tool" is refreshing and accurate. If only Mom would bring the same sound judgment to the other pressing issues affecting the marriage. Also, why didn't Mom come to check on Dad in the bathroom after, say, an hour?

MOM'S CAMPAIGN SPOKESWOMAN: Mom finds it telling that Dad has been unable to, so to speak, flush the toilets of the past, to metaphorically take off the porcelain lid and reach his hand down into the water and reattach the chain to the thingy. Instead, Dad prefers to revel in the relative glory of the bathroom incident over drinks at the local bar rather than to move forward and confront issues affecting the marriage today.

DAD'S CAMPAIGN SPOKESMAN: It is ironic for Mom to call on Dad to sever his ties with the Thirsty Bishop, a venerable neighborhood watering hole, since it was there, in 1986, that Dad realized he wanted to marry Mom. Consumed by love, Dad downgraded immediately from Budweiser to Pabst Blue Ribbon, and also stopped tipping, a sacrifice he was more than willing to make while he saved for an engagement ring.

MOM'S CAMPAIGN SPOKESWOMAN: Mom didn't know that.

DAD'S CAMPAIGN SPOKESMAN: Mom was all Dad could think about. Dad didn't quote poetry, like an East Coast elitist, or try to speak French, like a French guy visiting the East Coast, but expressed his love like a common American man, in tired clichés.

MOM'S CAMPAIGN SPOKESWOMAN: Mom remembers when Dad said, "You take my breath away," and Mom was startled, because his flushed complexion and hyperventilation suggested at first that he really wasn't getting enough oxygen.

DAD'S CAMPAIGN SPOKESMAN: Dad was wondering, if Mom isn't doing anything tonight, if she would care to discuss things directly, over a cup of coffee, without spokespersons.

MOM'S CAMPAIGN SPOKESWOMAN: Mom would like that.

DAD'S CAMPAIGN SPOKESMAN: To tell the truth, Dad doesn't even remember how the whole crazy fight got started.

MOM'S CAMPAIGN SPOKESWOMAN: On September third, after returning early from her night class, Mom walked in on Dad with Janine, the hot secretary, who was huddled close to him and gazing up with wide eyes, one of them shaped like an almond, the other like a pecan, asking, "Weren't you scared in the bathroom?"

DAD'S CAMPAIGN SPOKESMAN: Mom's characterization of Janine as a hot secretary is further evidence that Mom is out of touch with working Americans. Janine is a hot administrative assistant. As for Dad's fear and courage in the bathroom, his experience is well documented. As he wrote in his memoir, *Fantasizing About My Fathers:* "It was that day in the bathroom when my faith in God, which had eluded me in my arrogant youth, ascended to the realm of fact, for, had I been locked in any other room, I would surely, in the face of such hopelessness, have wet my pants."

I PROBABLY SHOULDN'T HAVE OPTED FOR THE CHEAPEST HMO

Jim Stallard

The Dermatologist

"All right, Jim, let's take a look at you here and see what you've got going . . . Oh my God." (*Vomits into wastebasket.*)

"The reason I didn't say anything to you before, smart guy, is that melanoma isn't contagious. Now, are you going to let me be the doctor?"

The Primary-Care Physician

"I didn't mean to laugh. I've just never seen this kind of muscle tone on a man before."

"The treatment won't work unless you're diligent about taking it. Did you hold the crystals in each hand for twenty minutes a day while facing north?"

The Radiologist

"Let me show you what we're up against. See the outline of this shadow in the upper-right quadrant of your lung? Ethically, I can't prescribe any treatment that would destroy the Virgin Mary."

"You don't have any metal in your body, do you? We just spent three hours cleaning out the MRI machine from our last patient."

The Urologist

"Wow, your prostate feels exactly like mine. Here, check it out."

"This has me stumped. Have you tried urinating just every other day? It's worth a shot."

The Gastroenterologist

"Put the earplugs in now, because I'm really gonna blast this. Tapeworms can't stand reggae."

"We need to boost your black bile so it's up to the level of your other three humors. Let me thread this doohickey up through your nostril."

The Surgeon

"We're going to put you under now, but you'll enjoy it. Once you get a whiff of this ether, you can't get enough—take it from me."

"The cone is just to make sure you don't bite at your suture and pull out the stitches. Nobody is going to notice it, I guarantee you."

PRESIDENTS WHO COULD ALSO BE STRIPPERS

Noel Wood

Madison
Taylor
Kennedy
Reagan

STATE RULES

Colin Perkins

Don't mess with Texas.
Don't flirt with Rhode Island.
Don't presume to tell Colorado about its business.
Don't stand so close to Mississippi.
Don't call Oregon after eleven.
Don't play your little games with Michigan.
Don't loan money to Maryland.
Don't you wish your girlfriend was hot like Kansas?
Don't you know who Georgia's dad is?
Don't even try to pay. This one is on Nevada.
Don't go changing to try and please Wyoming.
Don't look now, but there's Nebraska.
Don't act like you haven't been screening Vermont's calls.
Don't tell me you forgot about that night you spent in Maine.
Don't forget Utah's pills.
Don't be so quick to dismiss Arizona as a wacko.
Don't even touch Louisiana right now. Not after the stunt you just
    pulled.
Don't you go getting famous and forgetting all about Ohio.
Don't you have a friend you could hook Kentucky up with?
Don't give Connecticut the satisfaction of seeing you cry.

Don't look a South Carolina in the mouth.

Don't give Illinois any of your sass.

Don't come crawling back to Montana.

Don't get fresh with Florida.

Don't settle for Tennessee.

Don't go to bed angry at North Dakota.

Don't let New Hampshire get you down.

Don't forget to call Pennsylvania to say that you got home safe.

Don't you have anything to say to Washington for all the nice gifts?

Don't cry for me, Oklahoma. The truth is I never left you.

Don't get comfortable in Idaho.

Don't reckon you're from New Mexico?

Don't you feel guilty about Missouri?

Don't stop thinking about Wisconsin.

Don't speak. Iowa knows just what you're saying. So please stop explaining. Don't tell Iowa because it hurts.

Don't let Indiana catch you showing your face around here again.

Don't make Arkansas turn this car around.

Don't try to use reverse psychology on Minnesota.

Don't take West Virginia's picture.

Don't hate Hawaii because it's beautiful.

Don't put all your eggs in Delaware.

Don't drag Virginia into your drama.

Don't tell New Jersey you love it unless you really mean it.

Don't look directly at Alabama.

Don't look back at Massachusetts in anger.

Don't look to New York for advice.

Don't tell me you don't remember California.

Don't sweat the small Alaskan things.

Don't put off until tomorrow what you can do in North Carolina today.

Don't ever go to South Dakota for any reason.

GREAT QUOTES FROM THE END OF NASA'S SPACE SHUTTLE ERA

Jim Santel

"Houston, Tranquility Base here. The *Eagle* is wondering about the future of its dental benefits."

"We choose to privatize space travel not because it is easy, but because it is cost-effective and palatable to both political parties."

"To the International Space Station, and not beyond!"

"Godspeed, Space Camp application numbers."

"Houston, we have a problem: the Russians' reward program doesn't take our miles."

"That's one small concession to deficit realities, one giant blow to the dreams of children who want to be astronauts when they grow up."

THINGS JFK MIGHT ASK YOU TO ASK NOT TODAY

Kate Hahn

Can the country—and I mean rural America—do anything for me that this economically barren and increasingly crime-ridden decaying city cannot?

Should I just move to the country and find out?

Do too many people in the country have goat farms already? Like in Vermont? Or does it seem possibly like a viable way to earn a living?

What about an organic pie business?

Or making candles from my own beeswax?

How many acres of farmland would I need to feed myself? Just me. I don't have a family.

Can the country simultaneously exist as both a romantic pastoral ideal and an actual place if I go to live there? Or will I have to let go of this duality?

Does it show how overeducated I am?

How do I learn more about goats?

Are there a lot of government regulations when it comes to making small-batch organic artisan goat cheese, and are they enforceable?

How much postconsumer recycled material would I use in the packaging for the candles?

Will I get along with the people in the country, or will they shun me?

If one of my goats escapes and gets hit by a car, who is at fault?

How much do I really need for an organic fruit pie start-up?

Do goats get smallpox, and can they give it to humans?

Was that a gunshot or a truck backfiring? Or both a gunshot and a truck backfiring as the driver tries to escape the armed thieves stealing the cargo?

Is it fireworks? It is fireworks. Is it New Year's already? Has another year gone by? Really? Where have I been? What have I been doing? What have I accomplished?

Can you tell me when the next Greyhound bus is leaving for the country?

THE SONGS OF LENIN AND McCARTHY

Jimmy Chen

Lenin

"Still in the USSR"
"Baby, You're Not a Rich Man"
"Being for the Benefit of Mr. Marx!"
"All You Need Is State"
"Magical Bolshevik Tour"
"Paperback Propaganda Writer"
"Happiness Is a Cold War"
"Revolution"

McCarthy

"Here, There and Everywhere (Communists)"
"Everybody's Got Something to Hide, Period"
"Red Submarine"
"We Can't Work It Out"
"Blackbook"
"Your Father Should Know"
"Baby It's You"
"I've Got a Feeling"
"Hey Jew"
"Revolution 9"

FRAGMENTS FROM *WIKILEAKS!*
THE MUSICAL

Ben Greenman

Premiered: June 17, 2014
Performances: 31
Note: *This musical suffered somewhat from its proximity to* NOBEL!
THE MUSICAL, *which had opened a month prior and which also featured a protagonist driven to his adult fate by traumatic early embarrassment. The show also had an innovative marketing strategy that backfired: in the spirit of WikiLeaks, the producers created a website on which they released documents exposing the private lives of theater critics. One married critic was outed as gay; one gay critic was outed as straight; the resulting scandal hurt the show rather than helped it.*

{A playground, Australia, mid-1980s. Two girls are gossiping.}

SALLY

You know who I love?
That band Men at Work.
Did you hear of the scandal
With Annie and Dirk?
They were caught making out
By a school clerk

LISA

Someone told me. I think it was Lou.
They were over by the football ground
They were naked; she was making a sound
Like a hot and bothered kangaroo.

SALLY

I also heard that Mr. Nantz
Was driving his car without any pants

LISA

He's the one
With the red Impala?
He has tufts of hair
Just like a koala

{JULIAN ASSANGE approaches.}

SALLY

Uh oh, it's Julian
He's a little bit strange
Let's lower our voices
As he comes into range

LISA

I agree with you
This is not for his ears
We can start talking normal
When he disappears

{SALLY and LISA start to whisper.}

JULIAN ASSANGE

What are you guys
Talking about?

LISA

It's none of your business
Don't stick in your snout

JULIAN ASSANGE

But whispering is impolite
It's cliquish, mean, and just not right.
Your secrecy is a kind of slap.

LISA

You should tell someone who gives a crap

JULIAN ASSANGE

I don't like how this is going
My curiosity is growing.
Come on, tell me. Really, tell!
To not know is a kind of hell

{SALLY and LISA whisper more and then leave, giggling.}

JULIAN ASSANGE

I'll get you!
I'll get you!
Don't believe me?
I'll bet you!
There will be retribution!
There will be tit for tat!

There will be revolution
I will see to that!

{*Enraged and frustrated, JULIAN ASSANGE becomes a hacker. He devotes himself to the unchecked distribution of all information.*}

JULIAN ASSANGE

I'll dub myself Mendax
It means "noble liar."
I'll remake myself as a
High-tech town crier
When people attempt
To hide information
I will be the one
To compel revelation

{*After two decades moving between the hacking subculture and academia, JULIAN ASSANGE founds WikiLeaks, a website devoted to challenging secrecy regulations by releasing documents.*}

JULIAN ASSANGE

To radically shift regime behavior
We must accept a new kind of savior:
How can any authority control what we see
When all information wants to be free?

{*At first, JULIAN ASSANGE uses WikiLeaks for good, exposing assassinations in Kenya.*}

JULIAN ASSANGE

Witness how I used my network
To interfere with Kenyan wetwork.
It's hard to grasp this type of power

I liken it to Bentham's tower
He called it the Panopticon
It acted as a check upon
All who thought they were being observed
This is what we have long deserved.

{One day JULIAN ASSANGE is contacted by a man named BRADLEY MANNING.}

BRADLEY MANNING

Hello, I am Bradley Manning
I work in intelligence
I know you by your reputation
And frankly, sir, I have the sense
That my position in the army
Grants me special access to
Secret information that I
Think that I might leak to you.

JULIAN ASSANGE

What's your name, now? Manning? Bradley?
Tell me more; I'll listen, gladly.

{BRADLEY MANNING sends JULIAN ASSANGE video shot from an Apache helicopter flying over Baghdad and engaging in fire that results in the death of a dozen civilians. The video, which is titled Collateral Murder, *ignites a media firestorm. JULIAN ASSANGE even appears on* The Colbert Report.*}*

STEPHEN COLBERT

You say you are objective
But this title is incendiary
Tell me why, in light of that,

The rest of us should not be wary
Of your motives and your sympathies.
Are you the cure or a new disease?
This whole thing feels nefarious.

JULIAN ASSANGE

Ha ha, Stephen, you're hilarious.

{*BRADLEY MANNING, excited by the attention, contacts JULIAN AS-SANGE again and promises an even bigger set of leaks.*}

JULIAN ASSANGE

I'm a hacker, not a shrink
But something strikes me kind of funny
You're not doing this for fame,
Not exactly, not for money
So what, then, are your motives here?
Are you simply trying to right the scales?
Or is there a more deeply rooted
Reason to give up these details?

BRADLEY MANNING

What do you mean?
Do you posit that a leak
Is a way to open up
The closet, so to speak?

I hadn't thought it through
Though it comes as a relief
After years of dark, the light
Don't ask, do tell: that's my belief.
And what about you?
You must feel this way too.

{JULIAN ASSANGE nervously clears his throat.}

JULIAN ASSANGE

Well, look, don't think too much about it
I don't want to cause you aggravation

BRADLEY MANNING

No, no: I find it interesting
But what about your motivation?

JULIAN ASSANGE

What about my motivation?
Yes, indeed: a valid question
And one that after all these years
Still causes me indigestion
I can shift the course of nations
I can make great leaders cower
I can take pure information
And use it to disorder power
My reasoning for doing this
Isn't, I don't think, germane
Let's set aside this speculation
And go on with this great campaign

{JULIAN ASSANGE hangs up the phone quickly. ADVOCATES OF FREE INFORMATION hail JULIAN ASSANGE as a prophet.}

ADVOCATES OF FREE INFORMATION

That man is great
His site is greater
Society will
See that later.

He drinks in
Information, see,
And takes a leak
For liberty

{JULIAN ASSANGE leaks the more than 250,000 documents he has received, despite the arrest of BRADLEY MANNING.}

JULIAN ASSANGE

Once the world was benighted
Once the planet's eyes were closed
Now the earth has come awake
To all the facts that I've disclosed:
That flabby old chap Kim Jong-il,
Will be in the grave very soon.
Angela Merkel is rarely creative.
The U.S. spied on Ban Ki-moon.
Pakistan's stockpile of nukes
Isn't kept under lock and key.
The world now knows all these things
Because of me, because of me.

{Immediately, there is worldwide condemnation.}

HILLARY CLINTON

Diplomacy shaken, sources betrayed
Allies forsaken, leaders dismayed
This self-styled hero, this weasel Australian
Is the worst threat to freedom since Sarah Palin

GEORGE OSBORNE

It's a new dawn, a *nova aurora*,

Here is the box and here is Pandora
This kind of thing is a Hobson's choice
Do I really have a high-pitched voice?

VLADIMIR PUTIN

The way I'm being talked about
Fills me up with deep disquiet
That should concern the rest of you
Remember the Litvinenko diet?

NICOLAS SARKOZY

Much of what's in here
Is rumor and twaddle
Plus, what do I care?
My wife is a model.

ANGELA MERKEL

They say I don't like risk
And that I'm not creative
That is absurd,
As anyone can tell you.

{JULIAN ASSANGE is triumphant, even in the face of rape accusations from Sweden. He keeps on the run, living in airports and communicating mostly through online chats.}

JULIAN ASSANGE

I'm almost done, I'm almost done.
Just one more thing to do.
I made a promise years ago
And now I'll follow through

{SALLY, now in her thirties and living in America, is walking home from work. A black limousine pulls up alongside her. The window goes down. The DRIVER speaks.}

DRIVER

Excuse me, miss
Please define "inform"
While I knock you out
With this chloroform

SALLY

A cloth? A goon?
By my troth, I swoon.

{SALLY passes out and wakes in a room filled with computers. JULIAN ASSANGE is sitting in a black leather armchair, watching her.}

JULIAN ASSANGE

You can scream all you want
This room traps every sound

SALLY

Hey, you're that weird kid
From the middle-school playground.

JULIAN ASSANGE

The way I rub my hands together
Demonstrates that I am evil
The dark, malignant overlord
Of all information retrieval

I want you here now
To watch as I humble

The earth's greatest nations
Let them all crumble!

More importantly, Sally,
Let's settle a score
For years I have suffered
I will suffer no more.

Back in Australia
You and Lisa concealed
Information from me
I want it revealed

SALLY

Are you kidding or
Are you just insane?
Why would that stuff
Still be in my brain?
We were kids back then
A lifetime's passed.
I am shocked and stunned
Agog and aghast.

JULIAN ASSANGE

Seriously? You don't remember?
That's quite disappointing to hear
Lisa said the exact same thing
When I met her in Sweden last year

{JULIAN ASSANGE lets Sally go.}

JULIAN ASSANGE

Very sorry for the fuss.
Let's just keep this between us.

THE ELEMENTS OF PRESS RELEASE STYLE

Gary Klien

1. Omit needless words.

Vigorous writing is concise. A press release should contain no unnecessary words, for the same reason a drawing should have no unnecessary lines and a machine no unnecessary parts.

BAD

"The company regrets its role in this major environmental catastrophe, and we are fully committed to making the community whole."

BETTER

"This environmental catastrophe is regrettable."

2. Avoid the use of qualifiers.

Rather, very, little, pretty—these are the leeches that infest the pond of prose, sucking the blood of press releases.

BAD

"The chief executive officer's quite reasonable salary and benefits package reflects the rather challenging economic climate and the highly competitive market for top-flight management talent, under which the compensation committee was forced to operate."

BETTER
"The chief executive officer is undercompensated for the market."

3. Place yourself in the background.
Write in a way that draws the reader's attention to the substance of the press release, rather than to the mood and temper of management.

BAD
"This wrongful-death lawsuit is nothing more than a publicity stunt by bloodsucking extortionist trial attorneys for the benefit of their shiftless enablers in the news media."

BETTER
"While our thoughts and prayers are with Timmy's family at this difficult time, their claim is baseless and without merit."

4. Place the emphatic words of a sentence at the end.
BAD
"Aggressive outsourcing resulted in a 90 percent reduction in operating expenses, but after-tax profits still fell 37 percent year-over-year."

BETTER
"While profit fell short of expectations, our proactive restructuring initiative nearly doubled productivity."

5. Do not overwrite.
Rich, ornate prose is hard to digest, generally unwholesome, and sometimes nauseating. It is always a good idea to reread your writing later and ruthlessly delete the excess.

BAD
"The leadership is confident that its careful and prudent approach to the issue will increase prosperity for more American families in the long term."

BETTER

"We gutted the job-killing entitlement."

6. Do not overstate.

When you overstate, the press will constantly be on guard, and everything that preceded your overstatement as well as everything that follows it will be suspect in their minds.

BAD

"The local news and commentary site receives an estimated two million page views per minute, making our $400 million investment a veritable bargain for our stakeholders."

BETTER

"The blog deal is a stock play."

7. Revise and rewrite.

Revising is part of writing. Remember, it is no sign of weakness or defeat that your press release ends up in need of major surgery. This is a common occurrence in all writing, and among the best writers.

BAD

"Our internal investigation has pinpointed the blast origin to a defective part slated for replacement in 1975."

BETTER

"We are investigating the possibility of sabotage by eco-terrorists."

8. Avoid fancy words.

Do not be tempted by a twenty-dollar word when there is a ten-center handy, ready and able. Anglo-Saxon is a livelier tongue than Latin, so use Anglo-Saxon words. In this, as in so many matters pertaining to style, one's ear must be one's guide.

BAD

"We are carefully monitoring the FDA's response to widespread *Clostridium botulinum* and *Listeria monocytogenes* contamination in our products and are deeply troubled by reports of acute gastrointestinal hemorrhaging."

BETTER

"We stand by our line of organic, free-trade products."

9. Do not take shortcuts at the cost of clarity.

Do not use initials for the names of organizations or movements unless you are certain the initials will be readily understood.

BAD

"We are postponing our IPO in light of the SEC and CFTC investigations."

BETTER

"We are proud to be a privately held concern."

10. Do not affect a breezy manner.

The volume of press statements is enormous these days, and much of it has a sort of windiness about it. The breezy style is often the work of an egocentric person who imagines that everything that comes to mind creates high spirits and carries the day.

BAD

"Mission accomplished."

BETTER

"We are confident the humanitarian intervention was constitutionally sound, and deeply regret the civilian casualties resulting from our inadvertent annihilation of the farming village."

WHICH FLAVOR OF ICE CREAM
DO YOU WANT, DADDY?

Miles Kahn

Well, Malia, that's an excellent question. Now, you're going to be hearing a lot about flavors from a lot of different Americans in the coming months. And that's one of the reasons why this county is so great. From our first days on vacation, to where we are right now at Mad Martha's Ice Cream Shop, we have put our faith in free markets as the engine of America's resourcefulness. Together, we must rise to meet the responsibility of choice, be it vanilla, chocolate, or something more fruit-based.

These are more than just flavors on a cone. *Pistachio. Maple Nut. Black Velvet.* Ice creams ingeniously infused with all manner of dough, cookies, and confections. Americans have worked hard for them. Americans like Tom Baxt of Martha's Vineyard, Massachusetts. Now Tom, who stands directly behind me in line, told me just recently to "move it along, buddy." I believe we *can* move it along. And we will.

These are the flavors we've been waiting for. And yet, there are some in Congress right now who would rather see me choose the wrong ice cream than see America win. They claim that choosing Amaretto Chip would encourage a Euro-gelato ideology. Or that a preference for Rocky Road is just a partisan pitch to fund the House Transportation Committee. Nothing could be further from the truth.

The people behind me in line, shaking their fists in solidarity—some even yelling "choose, choose"—are testament to the importance of this day.

I think of Tom Carvel, whose development of advanced refrigeration technology brought us soft serve and our nation's Fudgie the Whale. I think of Americans like Burt Baskin and Irv Robbins, who in 1953 toppled Howard Johnson's twenty-eight-flavor benchmark. It is because of their entrepreneurial spirit, and the thousands like them, that we find ourselves staring at the precipice of over twenty flavors here at Mad Martha's, where a line of hungry, frenzied Americans continues to form behind me out the door.

I believe there are those in the Republican Party who find ice cream delicious. I'm eager to reach across the aisle and hear about other flavor and topping combinations that we've yet to explore. Are there fat-free ice creams that still maintain a full, creamy finish? Are there methods to meld candy bars and ice creams together into a unique new flavor? This is a goal we can and will achieve. Which is why I'm forming a bipartisan commission to research our options and put us back on track as a nation.

What's that? Waffle or sugar cone? Well, Sasha, that's an excellent question . . .

AESOP'S FABLES TEACH CHILDREN
THE ART OF VOTER SUPPRESSION

Andrew Golden

The little zebra was coming back to his ward of the savanna after doing some important errands, when an odd scene caught his eye.

His local polling place was packed. The lines were very long and overwhelmingly composed of tired, confused-looking antelopes.

At that moment, Mr. Giraffe whistled for the zebra to come over.

"Hey, Zebra," hissed Mr. Giraffe. "We need your help here! We're overwhelmed."

"Are you getting out the vote?" asked the zebra innocently.

"Are you kidding? No, we've got to win this thing, Zebra. BAMN. That's right, an acronym. 'By Any Means Necessary.' For the good of this savanna. Listen, put on one of these T-shirts."

"Why?" said the zebra, as he was handed a T-shirt with the phrase "Anti-Fraud Enforcement" written across the chest. He noticed that Mr. Giraffe and several menacing-looking hyenas were wearing them, too.

"Check out these antelopes, little Zebra," said the giraffe under his breath. "All looking for a free handout. And that music they listen to. Well, we're not gonna let them or their NAAAP thugs steal this from us. Here's what I want you to do. See that old antelope over

there? Tell her she's at the wrong polling place. Then, if she acts confused, tell her she needs to show you six forms of ID."

"But what about free elections?"

"That's cute," said Mr. Giraffe. He turned quickly around to see
a couple of young, idealistic-looking antelopes getting in line. "Hey,
guys, you know if you've got any outstanding parking tickets we're
going to have to arrest you if you check in to vote. *It's all right there
in the fine print.* And if you have any parking misdemeanors on your
record? You're going away for a long, long time."

The antelopes scattered away.

"This is illegal!" protested the zebra.

"You're illegal, Zebra. You're illegal. Shut the fuck up. I mean,
do you want 'Hanoi' Hippo to win this thing? If he gets in, the vampire bats win."

"I feel bad about this . . . " whined the zebra.

"You do what we tell you, or we'll take the tax exemptions away
from your synagogue! And another thing: if you see any born-again
rhinos come to this precinct, or any fat lions wearing 'Who Farted?'
T-shirts, send them to the front of the line. And give them eleven
ballots. I can't wait to read wild African jackass Bill Kristol's column
tomorrow!"

"Well," shrugged the young zebra. "At least I'll go to my grave
knowing that no cheetah couples ever gained hospital-visitation
rights or filed joint tax returns on my watch! Phew!"

THIS RECESSION HAS SPARED NO ONE, NOT EVEN THE MYTHICAL AND FOLKLORIC FIGURES OF OUR COLLECTIVE WESTERN IMAGINATION

Henry Alford and Ryan Haney

{Suburbia, 4:30 a.m. A YOUNG DAD, in his pajamas, stumbles sleepily out his front door and beholds the EASTER BUNNY. The EASTER BUNNY, slightly haggard-looking in a dishwater-gray tracksuit, is smoking a cigarette and scattering a dozen Costco eggs on the lawn.}

YOUNG DAD: Uh—don't you usually *hide* the eggs?

EASTER BUNNY: Cutbacks.

———

{A skirt-suited and bespectacled TOOTH FAIRY quietly flutters through the window of a small GIRL's bedroom. She takes an elastic band off her wrist and ties her wings back. Then she removes a plain white envelope from her briefcase.}

GIRL: Tooth Fairy! What's in the envelope?

TOOTH FAIRY: (*with a corporate crispness; over aspirated consonants*) A certificate of deposit.

GIRL: A what? (*She takes and tears open the envelope.*) Where's the cash?

TOOTH FAIRY: We found our last rewards program to be a bit reckless. But those seventy-five cents can be the first building block of a steady financial foundation.

GIRL: Seventy-five cents? I got five dollars for my last tooth!

TOOTH FAIRY: You'll be there in no time, dear. Interest rates should be way up by the time you need to roll that thing over in eighteen months.

GIRL: Can I just have the money now?

TOOTH FAIRY: I'd let it come to maturity if I were you. The withdrawal penalties can kill your Quarter 2.

———

{*SANTA CLAUS is standing next to a chimney, beside which sits his sack of gifts. He pulls three small gifts out of the sack and hands them to a snooty-looking elf INTERN.*}

SANTA CLAUS: I'll take this house, you do next door . . . Now, regarding display. You'll want to put the biggest gift out in front so it's the farthest away from the tree. Then put the next biggest gift behind that one, and then the smallest gift behind that one.

INTERN: This is so the family'll open the biggest box first?

SANTA CLAUS: No, this is to create the illusion of depth.

INTERN: Oh, a forced-perspective thing.

SANTA CLAUS: Yeah, okay, M. C. Escher—"a forced-perspective thing." Also, here's something that will help you with the stockings. (*Santa reaches into the sack and hands the intern a handful of packing peanuts.*) Volumizers.

INTERN: Do people really fall for this kind of thing?

SANTA CLAUS: (*glowering*) Don't fuck with me.

———

{*A perplexed ANGEL sees FATHER TIME decanting some of the sand from his hourglass.*}

ANGEL: Father Time, are you shortening time?

FATHER TIME: Indeed, Angel. The fifty-minute hour. It's psychiatrist-approved.

ANGEL: (*starting to sob*) You dare alter the fabric of existence so?

FATHER TIME: I do. I must. By the year 2825, the average human will be sixty-five by the third month of his life.

ANGEL: Even if he moisturizes aggressively?

FATHER TIME: Yes, my son. But this will not be my greatest legacy. My greatest legacy will be how I am going to alter the months of the calendar. From here on, the sequence shall run January, February, March, April, August, September, October, November, December— thus eliminating the middle, or "trash," months.

ANGEL: The world as I know it is coming to an end.

FATHER TIME: (*with false modesty*) Well, don't make me a folk hero.

ANGEL: Eons of human endeavor and thought, casually eradicated at the hands of a sole arbiter.

FATHER TIME: I'm always trying to cut a corner.

———

{The GRIM REAPER walks, almost floats, up the front steps of a brownstone. A single long skeletal finger emerges from somewhere inside his sleeve. As he presses the buzzer for apartment 6C, a shrieking darkness begins to swallow up the street behind him. He waits. Nothing. He buzzes again. Still nothing. He looks at the clipboard he's carrying and scans the intercom system to the side of the door. Frustrated, he buzzes rapidly and repeatedly, then depresses the buzzer for a twenty-three-second-long drone. He cups his hands to the sides of his hood and tries to peer through the side window. He unleashes a bone-rattling sigh, and then scribbles a note and affixes it to the door. The note reads, "Sorry we missed you."}

POLL: DO I FULLY UNDERSTAND THE CONCEPT OF MARGIN OF ERROR?

Ben Greenman

(SAMPLE SIZE = 1)

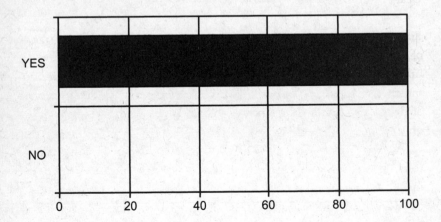

A LETTER FROM THE U.S. DEPARTMENT OF EDUCATION REGARDING THE BIRTH OF YOUR FIRST CHILD

Mark Brownlow

Dear Parent(s):

First of all, let us convey our sincerest congratulations on the birth of your son/daughter. Parenting brings both joy and great responsibility. The federal government believes that well-educated children must master certain standards to build a stronger nation. The future of the United States is now in your hands. Again, our warmest congratulations.

Within this packet, you will find twenty-six multiple-choice tests, as well as twenty-six corresponding Scantron answer documents and ten No. 2 pencils. You are to administer the tests to your child, one each week for the next six months. Toward the end of this six-month period, you will receive another packet, with tests for the following six months. The administration of these tests is of the utmost importance, for they will help us monitor your child's educational development. The tests must be completed by your child, then returned in the self-addressed envelopes also enclosed.

Take a few moments to glance through the tests. You will notice that each one has seventy-five questions, ranging from such basic concepts as letter recognition to more difficult items on advanced applied calculus and quantum physics. Please understand, your infant is not expected to answer every question correctly. The federal government is aware of the fact that very few infants, if any, will accurately complete the final problems of the assessment. Let us explain the rationale behind including these more challenging questions.

In the field of education, these tests are known as "benchmark assessments." By testing your child on concepts he or she has not yet mastered but will eventually be expected to master, the federal government can track your child's learning progress. A benchmark assessment will show exactly when your child has mastered a particular standard. In other words, although your infant will most likely be unable to determine the value of a variable in a pre-algebraic equation, by the end of first grade he or she will be expected to exhibit a competency in this area. And the good news is that by that time, your child's teacher will be administering the tests, not you. You are only responsible for the tests to be administered before your child enters an educational institute.

You may be wondering how the federal government will use these numbers. The scores your child receives will help determine his or her learning level. If your child scores very well, he or she will immediately be placed with other children who have attained a similar ranking. These children will be taught at an advanced pace, ensuring that the intellects of the most gifted students will not be neglected while the teacher painstakingly instructs the slower learners. The converse is also true. If your child is a slow learner, he or she will be consigned to an institute that serves the academically challenged, and he or she will be instructed at a remedial pace. This will guarantee your child an educational experience catering specifically to his or her particular needs.

If you have any reservations about this system, let us remind you that these are federally mandated requirements under the No Child Left Behind 2012 legislation, and they carry with them the weight of law. Any parent who does not conform to the letter of the law will find their federal funding, in the form of child tax credits, tax refunds, or government assistance in any form, immediately revoked. Also, any child of nonconforming parents will be barred from attending public school. Furthermore, if your child is consistently performing below a certain level on the tests, which would indicate that you, as a parent, are not preparing your child well enough for his or her future, the federal government has the right to take over the parenting of your child to ensure that his or her best educational interests are met.

One final note: federal test-administration monitors will occasionally drop by your house when it's time for that week's testing. Please welcome them and allow them to carry out their duties without obstruction.

Congratulations again on the birth of your first child! Together, you, as parents, along with the federal government, will create a better future for every child in this great nation.

Sincerely,
The United States Department of Education

IMPORTANT DETAILS ABOUT YOUR NEW HEALTH CARE PLAN

Dan Kennedy

The whole mess of us pass through customs, one big damp hot-house horde, families on vacation, middle-aged spiritually bankrupt desperadoes, young devil dolls from Los Angeles all gasoline blood, hot-rod giggle, and summer snatch that almost nobody on earth is having until the curtain starts to come down on these girls like it comes down on all of us eventually to level the field and narrow the options. The whole parade of us moves along like time-lapse photography; eventually everyone will go through one of three narrow gates with glass booths at the end. The passport gets slipped under and stamped; the questions are asked. Why are you here? Just say "vacation." And by vacation, I mean having around nine thousand tiny sonic thumps aimed at the right kidney until you're able to piss bloody sand on this blue-lagoon heaven, then get on a plane bound back to American airspace. Shuffle along now, the dull pain lurch-and-drag, right past the suckers who checked bags. Your small backpack and carry-on bag turn out to be targets for a hustle-and-grin shakedown. Two rather official-looking men will likely run up all smiles; they want money to carry it five or ten feet to the front door for you. It'll probably go like this:

"I carry, we carry, sir."

"I'm not . . . I can . . . no."

"Thank you, yes, we carry, please!"

"Fuck, the," you say while yanking the backpack right back from Nusa, or Naruda, Akimbo, Gurn Blanston, Mondo Paw, Frond Jewel, or whatever parents named these grifters when they were still angels with dreams.

"Thank you. Please. To carry now for you," they keep saying at you.

"Fuck away. You dicking . . . up the?"

The one laugh the heart can count on is when the brain and mouth jumble out a weird little frightened and rushed stab at casually assertive profanity like this. Your face will try to sell it with a look, a look that tries to say, "Yes, that's right, you heard me: Fuck away you dicking up the."

The price of the cabs outside makes up for what one suffers to get to them; the prices are so low they seem unfair to the men driving them. The bags go in, smiles of teeth that have seen some miles, fair-price guarantees, a bunch of greetings. *Slam, swack, kerrang,* and the trunk, one door, then the second, closing shut hard in a zip of getting down to business. Up the airport drive, out the exit and onto what's left of the main drag, too skinny to take the punishment of traffic that has doubled yearly since Bush's second term. The proof of being so far from home arrives around the first bend in the pale and cracked tarmac vein, in the form of the endless smoky buzz-swarm of a thousand mopeds and motorbikes: one metallic brittle that breaks and scatters like mercury for narrow bottlenecks and anything big that's about to drift over into its lane. The bikes scurry right along at pace with the vans and cabs, smaller but fearless, like a rain of flies following elephants.

Checking into the hotel resort situation, you're swarmed again, this time by beautiful local women. They'll have drinks on little teak trays, cool cucumber towels in little bowls made of antler or bone. Not having health care is not that bad when you can make it to a place like this for the same price as heading down to St. Vincent's Hospital on Seventh Avenue back home before it went bankrupt and closed. That hospital stands there now like a fifteen- or twenty-story chimney of ghosts at the end of Eleventh Street in New York City. The only catch to not having health insurance in America is that you have to drink enough to pony up for the ticket on debt at LAX, but that's a system right there, so basically speaking, America's health care system is working just fine for you on this day. The paperwork in front of you is more fun to fill out when you don't have health insurance; it comes over with keys to a hotel suite, in a discreet little leather binder that has no idea just how low the balance at the bank has dipped after buying a plane ticket in white-hot pain at the very last minute, the night you were in LAX to fly home—that's when the pain started coming on worse than any of the other times over the last couple weeks. Here's the thing about the bank balance: it may be gone; in the red; in brackets; into the overdraft protection with its interest, fangs, fees, and slimy coked-up, slicked-back, anything-you-need-now-you-can-pay-for-later demeanor. The discreet and tasteful leather binder is opened, the confidence is screwed up, the paperwork signed, and an entourage of orange sarongs walks you to a huge upgrade so you can check in and check out for a while.

Lonely from twenty-three hours of flights, one tends to go about Googling ex-girlfriends or -boyfriends and stomach parasites you can get in India and Indonesia, stopping only to refocus the eyes by peeking out the window blinds for a moment. The eyes relax into a long focal length to stare at a luxurious white-sand beach littered with vacationers from America and the south coast of Australia. It's hard to figure who is here on kidney vacation and who is here on regular vacation. Everyone lies in the late-afternoon sun, enjoying drinks brought to them by waiters who stand by attentively in tuxedos abbreviated in the leg and length to accommodate the hot weather. Gazing upon the vacationers, it's easy to get the impression that Googling stomach viruses and quietly draining the minibar alone in hopes of killing pain is not how one is supposed to spend one's time here.

Before the haze turns to sleep, you'll want to make a call to the concierge so that a shuttle ride will be scheduled for tomorrow's appointment at BIMC Hospital, Nusa Dua. In a weird way, everything is working out just fine. The plane tickets, this hotel, the hospital tab, someone hanging around outside your hotel room and waiting on your every whim afterward; a driver to the hospital, to the hotel, and eventually back to the plane—it's all still about half the price of the kind of cash you'd lay out for two days in a hospital back home. And if you're self-employed, it's also way less than the insanely high insurance premiums you'd have paid during the time it took for this to go wrong inside you.

You're probably technically bankrupt at the moment, at least cash-wise. But the air-conditioning is on, there's a huge flat-screen television showing game shows out of Jakarta or Kuala Lumpur dubbed over poorly in English, and they crack you up on codeine, these shows—they really make you laugh. Sit back and relax, because you'll get back to America soon enough to be briefly and mildly over-paid, and it will be enough to make you think everything is going to work out fine. Plus, if anything goes wrong with you again, you can come back here. There's a girl down the hall who knows who you are; says she's read or heard or seen something you did. Plus, the bleeding is stopping, and you're even a little thinner from not being able to eat much during this stuff and in the weeks leading up to it. You have to admit, you feel pretty good. Hell, you feel kind of amazing. You feel like you're finally living the American Dream.

ROBERT GIBBS'S DUNGEONS & DRAGONS GAME GOES OFF THE RAILS

Travis Watt

Okay, Helen Thomas's thief rolled a seventeen on her Search roll, so your adventuring party enters the catacombs while the empty eye sockets of the skulls leer from the walls. Are we clear on this? The emptiness leers. It's a solid absence.

There's a hiss and a glug of a drain unclogging. Green bile boils up from invisible vents in the floor, catching everyone unaware. I'm sorry, but how do you know the vents are invisible? Because you can't see them. Are they magically invisible?

Perhaps. Then how come MSNBC's magic detect spell didn't detect any magic? Um, because they're not magic? How about that? Do you have a more pertinent question?

You're monitoring a very fluid situation. With the acidic, mystical bile.

No, I'm sorry, Chip Reid, the androsphinx-bladder boots you're wearing do not neutralize the bile's magic. That really only works, uh, on thaumaturgic hexes. This is a necromantic rite. Uh, I'm sorry, disregard that.

So remember: you can't remember that the bile is necromantic in nature. Forget that, I'm sorry. That's meta-gaming.

Chip, I know that the *Monster Manual* says the androspinx bladders protect against all ritualistic magic, but the manual means to preclude necromancy from that list. Necromancy's its own school of magic, after all. Let's not be unreasonable.

Remember, everyone, your characters can't remember that I said the bile is magical, nor specifically necromantic. Nor a rite.

Okay, so, everyone who is wearing less than full plate takes twelve points of damage. If you're wearing full plate, roll a d20, with a result of five or less indicating the bile has corroded your armor to a point of extreme fecklessness. How come you don't get a saving throw? That's the nature of the magic bile.

Jake Tapper, sorry, but your barbarian's Wasteland Perseverance feat doesn't get you a reroll on your saving throw against the bile. No, that particular feat doesn't—if you read the *Player's Handbook,* actually—that particular feat doesn't protect against magical hardships. Just alchemical threats.

I'm sorry? I've been as clear as I can: the magic bile is not magic.

No. No one in the press room gets rerolls. No one. I haven't invoked Dungeon Master's fiat, so no one gets to reroll. No. You all do take that damage. Yes, you do, Major Garrett, yes, you do. You're not going to? Fine. No, fine.

All right, everyone? Roll under your character's base Constitution. Do it now. Everyone adds eight because of the corrosive magic bile. No, Major, you don't have time to cast Reanimate Bones on the leering skulls with the empty eye sockets. Maybe if Helen Thomas had a better Search roll for an eleventh-level Halfling thief.

Did everyone roll under their Constitution? No one did? Good, then. Everyone's body is woven out of living pain as the bile detumesces everyone's skeleton. Except for your skulls.

Context clues, guys. That's why the catacombs' walls had skulls on them. Yes, your characters are dead. Next question? Yes, that is how you use the word *detumesce* in a sentence. Yes, it is. Yes, it is. It means, uh, to deflate. Yes. All right. You don't know the rules to this thing. You couldn't tell a gnoll from a gnome. You need to find a new DM. And I bet whoever you find will use Attacks of Opportunity. That's when a party of orcs can slaughter high-level characters, but whatever.

THE LABORS OF UNEMPLOYED HERCULES

Luke Burns

With the help of his dad, Hercules landed a job interview with a dangerous and crafty sphinx. To prepare, Hercules spent hours bench-pressing logs from redwood trees and carefully going over his suit with a lint roller. He felt certain that the job was as good as his.

"So, Mr. Hercules," said the sphinx, "after looking over your résumé, I was wondering: What walks on four legs in the morning, two legs in the afternoon, and three legs in the evening?"

Hercules let forth a hardy laugh. "Ha! That's easy! The answer is 'man.'" Hercules knew the answer because he had seen a list of commonly asked riddles asked by HR personnel on LinkedIn.

"Excellent," said the sphinx. "My next riddle is this: Your main qualification seems to be that you are very strong. Why do you think you'd make a good data entry clerk?"

Hercules did not get the job, and he narrowly avoided being eaten by the sphinx.

———

Hercules traveled to the very bottom of the world to see if he could pick up some part-time work helping Atlas, whose job was carrying the sky on his shoulders. The pay wasn't great, and Atlas didn't get any time off, but he did have a good benefits package.

"Hey, Atlas," said Hercules, "if you ever need someone to cover for you, I can take that off your back for a little bit."

"I'd love a break," Atlas grunted, "but if I cut back on my hours, I'll lose my health insurance." Atlas needed a lot of expensive medication to treat his chronic back pain and seasonal affective disorder.

Atlas sighed. "It's a job."

———

Thwarted at every turn, Hercules decided to take an internship with King Augeas. His first assignment was to clean out the king's enormous and filthy stables.

"Ha!" laughed Hercules. "I shall prove my worth by cleaning out these stables in *one day*! Then they'll be sure to hire me!" Hercules diverted a roaring river, and the powerful waters swept the muck from the stables in mere hours. Hercules triumphantly went to tell the king of his accomplishment.

"Wow, I thought that would take you way longer," said the king. "Jeez. Um, hang tight while I see what else there is for you to do . . ."

Hercules spent the rest of his internship getting coffee from the deli next to Augeas' castle.

———

After losing his apartment and moving to Mount Olympus to live with his dad, Hercules was forced to withstand a seemingly endless barrage of criticism.

"Why can't you be more like your brother Hermes?" Zeus asked. "He's doing really well in that messenger service."

"Well, Hermes has golden sandals that give him the power of flight," said Hercules. "It's easy to find a job if you can fly."

"You should have taken that job pushing a boulder up a hill for Sisyphus."

"I told you, Dad, that job sucks. Every time you get the boulder to the top of the hill, it rolls back down and you have to start all over again."

"I think you would have been good at it. And you like doing stuff with heavy things."

"I don't want to push the same boulder up the same hill my whole life," muttered Hercules.

"If you're not even going to *look* for a job, at least get out of the house a little bit. You know, turn into a swan or bull and meet some girls."

"Dad, I'm not like you. *I* can't turn into a swan!"

Zeus just shook his head and went out to the garage to tinker with his lightning bolts.

TEMPLATES TO THE EDITOR

Bob Woodiwiss

Blah-blah-blah

To the Editor:

Citation of a recent front-page story reporting on a national political issue. Statement of disbelief. Statement of indignation. Statement of disgust. Statement of arguable relevance and negligible value. Opinion asserted as fact. Certainty presented as reality. Brusque dismissal of any who would disagree. Bitter expression of pity for America's future.

    Patrician name
    Southern city

Same old story, same old denial

To the Publisher, Managing Editor, and All Citizens:

Declaration of great pride in holding elected office. Grudging acknowledgment of personal centrality in a nascent scandal of an ethical and/or sexual nature. Unsworn oath denying all charges, any wrongdoing. Doleful expression of familial pain being unjustly borne. Futile appeal not to rush to judgment. Feeble reminder of principle of presumed innocence. Aspersions cast on accusers. Unconvincing, unrealistic prophesy of complete exoneration.

Prominent name from last election cycle's yard signs
Everywhere

Elusive logic

To the Editor:

Brief articulation of a recognized societal problem. Highly selective facts about the problem. Oversimplification of root causes of the problem based on selective facts. Faulty conclusion based on oversimplification. Impractical solution based on faulty conclusion. Confident presumption of problem's eradication based on unlikely implementation of suggested impractical solution.

Common baby boomer first name, five-letter-noun last name
Inconsequential midwestern town

Unmade counterpoint

Editor:

Grievance concerning a syndicated op-ed column. Denunciation of the columnist's point of view and entire body of work. Self-important but unsubstantiated personal data and/or experience meant to lend authority to next sentence. Refutation of columnist's documented fact with fact pulled out of ass. Clumsily phrased and in all probability plagiarized analogy or metaphor. Generalized antipathy.

Arbitrary name
McMansion high-density area

Life isn't fair. We get it.

To the Editor:

Condensed recounting of a personal tragedy involving a family member, close friend, or professional colleague. Perceived injustice of the tragedy, stopping just short of blaming an indifferent deity. Dubious linkage of the small personal story to a larger, topical story. Step that must be taken by heretofore uninterested, untouched parties in order to prevent the same or similar tragedy from happening to them. Mawkish close re-mentioning victim's first name and sad plight.

> Non-household name
> Ignored corner of the world

Another economic genius

To the Editorial Board:

Reference to a recent editorial on a governmental budget issue. High-handed dismissal of the piece's suggested tax increases (or spending cuts) as counterproductive. Polarizing assertion that, conversely, spending cuts (or tax increases) are the requisite action. Specious economic parallel or example. Casting of suspicion on the motivations of all who would disagree. Curt close.

> Name with a middle initial
> A town like any other

Liberally conservative and vice versa

Sirs:

Boilerplate indictment of newspaper management for unfailingly allowing its political views to color news reporting. Pointed allegation as regards latest egregious example of story-embedded partiality. (Parenthetical aside listing smaller but still serious examples that did not escape attention.) Impartation of information gleaned from a separate, single, openly partisan source. High-minded conclusion that omitting this biased information proves the newspaper's bias. Huffy yet world-weary disappointment in the mainstream media's betrayal of the public trust.

Name that sounds like two first names
Where such people live

Frightened fearmonger

Editor:

Reference to recent violent inner-city-crime story. Lamentation over continual decay of urban core. Veiled racial slur. Account of personal municipal-crime story and unsatisfactory resolution. Veiled racial slur. Pledge to avoid entering city in perpetuity.

Name that does not end with a vowel other than *e*
Newer suburban city established as a white alternative to an older urban environment

I'm desperately lonesome

To the Editor:

Statement establishing perusal of a particular human-interest piece. Obligatory thank-you. Petty quibble with the depiction of an entirely inconsequential element of the piece. Flat, pointless anecdote based on a misremembered and romanticized past. Puzzling tangent casting doubt upon letter writer's ability to reason and/or ability to function in the world as well as the credulity and/or perspicacity of the Letters Editor. Almost pitiable attempt at wit.

Name that needs changing
A place you've never been

Overidentify much?

To the Editor:

Expression of outrage or elation inspired by a professional sports team's performance. Declaration of civic or personal mortification or pride as a result of the outcome. Forceful condemnation or unqualified praise of team ownership, players, and/or attending fans. Pledge of total disinterest in or unmitigated support for the team's future efforts. Optional: Never again or Go, [professional sports team name]!

Ignorable name
Wherever

SLIGHTLY LESS-CITED SUPREME COURT PRECEDENTS

Rob Kutner

Brown v. Board of Edutainment

Plessy v. Ferguson 2: 2 Separate 2 Equal

Kramer v. Kramer (not the divorce case, a schizophrenic episode for Seinfeld's neighbor)

Giant Rich Polluting Eating Corporation v. Tiny Hippie Quinoa Farm, LLC

Alien v. Predator (appealed from lower court)

What the Heart Wants v. What the Heart Married

Man v. Nature

Bob v. Carol v. Ted v. Alice

Darren v. Darren v. 10,000 Stand-Up Comics

Our Lady of the Gun-Toting Jesus v. Karl Marx's House of Gay-bortions

Joe v. T. Volcano

Long Shapeless Black Judicial Robes v. Electric-Blue Ab-Sculpting Unitards

Ross v. Wilson, McGlown & Ballard (later Birdsong)

Marbury v. Madison: LIVE on Pay-Per-View!

Chief Justice Holmes v. Huge Tin of Taffy He Should Not Have Consumed the Eve Prior

ARCHAIC U.S. SENATE PROCEDURES

Lucas Klauss

The Filibuster

The Clobberknob

The Scrummelduck

The Haffenwasky

The Packalackitt

The Delaware Dipsydoo

The Speckled Rooster

The Old Grumpy Swordfish

Aunt Regina's Slap-Yourself Pie

The Irish Filibuster

The {Sexist Epithet}

The {Racist Slur}

The {Very Racist Slur}

The {Possibly Anti-Masonic Reference}

The Satanic Filibuster

Daniel Webster's Reanimated Corpse

The Mighty Djinn and His Fellows

The Beast That Slumbers 'Neath the Aisles

The John McCain

The Bipartisan Vote

The Frilly Duster

CONGRESSIONAL MISSED CONNECTIONS

Sloan Schang

You: Sexy Filibuster Brown. Me: Shrinking junior member in the last row. Your recitation of whole episodes of *Murder, She Wrote* was brilliant. Didn't want it to end but I fell asleep in hour sixteen and when I woke up, you were gone. :-(E-mail me, I want to hear what matters to you.

———

Senate Dining Room last week, you were eating with some old guys and you caught me looking at you, lol. Was that bow tie for real? Dying to know.

———

Getting our shoes shined together and I was coveting your tawny Fratellis. Wanted to talk about redistricting but you said that's for behind closed doors. Can't stop thinking about that.

———

Me: Dashing salt-and-pepper Rep. yelling at an aide in the hallway.
You: Ravishing housewife on a tour of the chamber last Tuesday. I'm
not really that scary. Send a pic so I know it's you.

———

Am I crazy or were you were looking right at me every time you said
"two-party system"? Tell me I'm not crazy over coffee.

———

After Appropriations yesterday you proposed forming a "subcommit-
tee to kill some brain cells." Sounds more like a caucus to me. Where
do I sign up?? :)

———

You met with me in your office last month; I was the one worried
about losing my job. That smile looked like more than just "being
friendly to your constituents." Well, I lost my job, but maybe I
gained a friend (you)? It's probably a shot in the dark if you'll ever
read this but my fingers are crossed anyway. Like you said, things
have to start going my way sometime, right? Let me know.

CHAPTER TITLES FOR RACHEL CARSON'S 1962 BOOK *SILENT SPRING* THAT WERE REJECTED FOR BEING TOO ALARMIST

Caredwen Foley

"Slow Mercury Poisoning Giving You Amnesia and Causing You to Forget Your Mortgage Payment"

"Having Your Retinas Disintegrate from Too Many UV Rays and Finding Out the Tough Way That Your Girlfriend Is a Man"

"Phosphoric Acid Seeping into the Water Supply, Destroying Your Teeth, Leading to Your Dentist Telling You You Need a Root Canal"

"Getting Fired for Distributing 'Leftist Propaganda' About the Effects of Global Warming and Losing Your Dental Coverage Just in Time for the Aforementioned Root Canal"

FRAGMENTS FROM *HOT PLANET!*
THE MUSICAL

Ben Greenman

Premiered: May 6, 2014
Performances: 219
Note: *Al Gore played himself as an adult. Producers were opposed to the idea, but Gore wrote an impassioned plea in the form of a* New York Times *op-ed where he argued that no actor could communicate his "trademark mix of awkwardness and ideological passion." To everyone's surprise, he was wonderful in the role and earned a Tony nomination. He lost the award to Danny DeVito, who was playing Quint in a musical version of* Jaws.

———

{*It is the early 1960s. The Beatles have just invaded America. Early Motown spills from a car radio. The streets are filled with the delirious energy of young people liberated from the rigors of postwar thinking. The TEEN-AGED AL GORE goes to the beach.*}

TEENAGED AL GORE

I wish I could swim
See that boy over there?

I envy him so
He has such nice wet hair

But something arrests me
And gives me great pause
It's not fear of drowning
Not sharks, with their jaws.

I know the statistics
For all of these things
But the water is freezing
The freakin' stuff stings

{ANNA, also a teenager, hears TEENAGED AL GORE talking.}

ANNA

I am a girl of some repute
I have a low-cut bathing suit
I think that young Al Gore is cute
Last year in band I played the flute

{ANNA walks to the water. TEENAGED AL GORE starts to follow, but only takes a few steps into the water.}

TEENAGED AL GORE

Damn it
I'm shivering
My forearms are quivering
I wanted some bravery
But my heart's not delivering
Anna, wait—
You look great—
Sometimes males and females mate.

{ANNA looks at TEENAGED AL GORE.}

ANNA

Your lips are blue
And could use some pinking
But if I were you
I would mind the shrinking

{ANNA points theatrically toward the site of the shrinking. TEENAGED AL GORE covers himself. ANNA walks off with another boy.}

TEENAGED AL GORE

I curse this foul ocean
And its frigidity
Now I am left alone with
My own faint rigidity

I call on the gods
I ask them to decree
That the cold ocean turn
To a vast lukewarm sea

I call on the gods
To heat up the oceans
And by doing so save me
From my shameful emotions

{TEENAGED AL GORE goes home and tries to forget about ANNA. Three years later, when "What Becomes of the Brokenhearted" is a hit, he is still not cured of his heartbreak. He throws himself into his studies, then into journalism, then into politics. He marries. He starts a family. Years later, as a United States senator whose work concerns climate change, among other topics, AL GORE finds himself dictating an editorial for The Washington Post *to his secretary.}*

AL GORE

It's with a heavy heart that I enter this debate
Living species are expiring at a rapid rate
So here, right now, today, I call for a new plan
To rescue our dear earth from the tentacles of man
Perhaps around the Capitol you've seen my new graffiti:
"Big Al Says Let's Not Forget to Ratify the Kyoto Treaty."

{AL GORE goes home. He plays tennis, takes a little run, eats, watches an episode of ALF, and then steps into the shower, where he reflects with pride upon his editorial.}

AL GORE

It's a wonderful feeling
To take a hot shower
But the earth must be cooled in this perilous hour
I can wash, I can lather
I can rinse and repeat
But we must force this warming to beat a retreat

{Suddenly, in the shower, AL GORE stops still.}

AL GORE

Holy moly
Holy crap
It's as if
I got a slap

I remembered
Something bad
Back from when
I was a lad

{AL GORE goes into his bathroom and speaks to the mirror. He is nude.}

AL GORE

I have said that I don't know
The cause of global warming
That is not exactly true
I am partly disinforming

A few minutes ago
I was gripped by a thought
I was in a cold sweat
Though the water was hot

I was seized by the fear
That I caused this alarm
Years ago, as a boy
I did the earth harm

I was simply attempting
To turn a girl's head.
I didn't want boiling oceans
Or our polar bears dead!

I just wanted to walk
To the water and wade
But the ocean was cold
And I was far too afraid

{Consumed with guilt that his appeal to the gods caused the oceans to heat up, AL GORE devotes himself to an aggressive environmental agenda throughout his time as vice president in the Clinton administration. After losing the 2000 election to George W. Bush, AL GORE decides to exit politics and become a full-time climate-change activist.}

AL GORE

I fight for my planet every day

Like a kind of superhero
If climate change were a giant moth
I would be the great Gojira
That's Godzilla's real name
The two beasts are one and the same.

*{OTHERS question AL GORE's conclusions—not those regarding Godzil-
la, but those regarding climate change.}*

OTHERS

You say the planet's slowly heating
But honestly, aren't you repeating
Science that has been debunked
And consequently should be junked?

For that matter, suppose the seas
Are warmer by a few degrees—
Is this really something that
We must spend billions to combat?

*{AL GORE stands in front of a world map, which begins to scroll behind
him, and reviews what he has learned about climate change.}*

AL GORE

Look, I wore a Speedo
When I went to Tallinn
It's as warm as Quito
And that's just appalling

The very next day
It was off to Helsinki
Where I sported a thong
As wide as my pinky

Reykjavík was next

And to reprise my point
I fashioned a sleeve
To fit over my joint

In all of these places
It should have been freezing
But instead the weather
Was mild and pleasing

So when the detractors
Question this finding
I must always insist
That the facts here are binding

{After AL GORE's World Swimwear Tour, he invents a better way to spread his message: slide presentations on campuses across the country.}

AL GORE

Let me say right away
That my tone is monotonous
Still, you can see that
The earth will grow hot, and thus

We need to be careful
Be better caretakers
Consumers and companies
And even lawmakers

I know that some people
Think I'm Chicken Littling
But they are like Nero
While the earth warms, they're fiddling

{When people in the audience fall asleep, as some do, they blame it on the warm room, and blame that, in turn, on climate change. But, increasingly, people begin to show interest in AL GORE's work, including a number of celebrities.}

LAURIE DAVID

Am I upset?
Of course I am. You bet.
I'm also quite saddened and disturbed.
Our ability
To take responsibility
Has been almost completely curbed.

LEONARDO DiCAPRIO

We have to save our planet
We don't have any choice
We have an obligation
To speak with a collective voice
Until now all attempts
Have been tangled in red tape
Now I think I know
What's wrong with Gilbert Grape

{Different celebrities get different reactions from AL GORE.}

AL GORE

Absolutely—
Whatsoever—
So nice of you—
Right, yeah, whatever

JESSICA ALBA

Mr. Gore
I implore
You to let me do my part
Please, sir, tell me how to start
Do you need any help
Applying for new grants?

AL GORE

New studies have shown
What I have long known
Most of the warming
Occurs in my pants

{AL GORE and his celebrity supporters begin to spread the word about climate change. While talking to LEONARDO DiCAPRIO about whether This Boy's Life *should have carried a disclaimer distinguishing it from the magazine of similar name, AL GORE is approached by a HOLLYWOOD INSIDER.}*

HOLLYWOOD INSIDER

Excuse me
Mr. Vice President
I know
It's not so evident
But I love our environment
I'm conservationist. I'm green.
Have you thought of bringing
Your message to the silver screen?

AL GORE

I have, to be frank
It would help spread the news
I'm assuming that
I would be played by Tom Cruise?

HOLLYWOOD INSIDER

To illustrate your deep conviction
We were thinking a nonfiction
Film might make a bit more sense.
Plus, Cruise is handsome. No offense.

{AL GORE cries a bit but recovers his composure. The film, An Inconvenient Truth, *wins an Academy Award. AL GORE begins to fly around the world, spreading his message of climate change. Critics, including conservative commentator SEAN HANNITY, question his motives.}*

SEAN HANNITY

Brand him as a hypocrite?
Sure, I'll take a crack at it.
Can you believe that guy's presumption?
He preaches limited consumption
And energy awareness, yet
He travels in a private jet.
He's blinkered, unhinged, and pedantic
And his carbon footprint is gigantic

{AL GORE soldiers on.}

AL GORE

Other men fret about the economy
Or sharpen up their political bonhomie
Confronted with science that is large and complex
They put their heads in the sand and save their own necks

They say that I am grandstanding
Though my speeches now run a hundred grand
Still, how can you put a price on life
As our planet fights its brave last stand?

{Rumors begin that AL GORE may be awarded the Nobel Peace Prize. Finally, in October 2007, he is.}

AL GORE

The Peace!
The Prize!

What underlies
This great award
Is broad accord
On our earth's dire fate
The challenge for us now is great
Let's stand against waste and excess
And save our planet from distress

The Prize!
The Peace!
Can we decrease
Our consumption?
Our assumption
Is that we can
And offset the effects of man
We've walked the earth for centuries
Can't we tread more lightly, please?

The Peace!
The Prize!
The world's eyes
Are on this cause
Perhaps new laws
Will soon be passed
To help control our greenhouse gas
Emissions and pollution, too
Planet Earth, this one's for you!

{The lights fall. AL GORE speaks softly.}

AL GORE

The Prize!
The Peace!
I am released
From servitude

I feel renewed
When I was young I loved a girl
And thus endangered the whole world
I've done my penance; I've done my best;
I've acted nobly; now I can rest.

{AL GORE falls to his knees and kisses the earth. It is cooler than he expects. He smiles, closes his eyes. When he opens them, though, he is displeased. The celebrities have deserted him, and fewer people seem to believe in climate change as an absolute. AL GORE simmers for a year, then decides that his simmering is contributing to global warming. By that point, most of the American public has moved on to other issues: immigration, the economy, homeland security. Just after the tenth anniversary of 9/11, he plans a twenty-four-hour media event to draw attention to the planet's plight. It is likened to the Muscular Dystrophy Telethon, and AL GORE is likened to Jerry Lewis. He doesn't like the comparison, because he thinks that it's a veiled way of saying that his face is fat.}

RECYCLE, COMPOST, OR TRASH? A GUIDE

Jenny Shank

Welcome. As a citizen of a "zero waste" community, you must learn how to distinguish between items that may be recycled or composted and those that must, regrettably, be placed in the trash.

You will be charged by the kilogram for your personal weekly trash, which will be bundled and labeled with your name and address. In the event that our town landfill exceeds capacity, your past trash will be returned to you.

Plastic Lids

Flat lids on plastic containers (cottage cheese containers, salad containers, etc.) cannot be recycled. The sorting equipment sensors "read" these items as paper, not plastic, and they end up in the wrong bin. But some lids are made of corn and can be composted. To determine if your lid is compostable, take a bite.

Expired Prescription Drugs

To prevent drugs from entering the water supply or being used for illicit purposes, open the container and mix well with one cup of kitty litter and two tablespoons of coffee grounds. Then urinate on them, reseal, and dispose.

Lightbulbs
What color is your lightbulb? What shape? What wattage? Halogen, incandescent, or compact fluorescent? Is it broken or intact? If you are unable to answer all of these questions, you haven't earned the right to part with your lightbulb.

Old Sweaters
Why not have a yard sale?

Athletic Shoes
Did you know that athletic shoes can be turned into a material used to resurface athletic fields, tracks, and playgrounds? But the shoes must have no cleats, metal parts, zippers, or mud, and they may not be Keds-type canvas sneakers. Only 1985–1989 Air Jordans will be accepted.

Plastic Bags
No. 2 and No. 4 plastic bags: recyclable. No. 3 and No. 5 plastic bags are compostable, but No. 6 and No. 8 plastic bags must be trashed. There is no such thing as a No. 7 plastic bag.

Newspapers
You still subscribe to the newspaper? That's cute.

Used Mattresses
Fasten to the top of your car with twine and drive it to the Center for Hard-to-Recycle Materials on the outskirts of town. Go past the mountain of old tires and the pit of Unflushable Things That Were Nevertheless Flushed, and take a left. About sixty yards down the road, you will find our community's mattress heap, guarded by two Gorgons, Argus, and a pit bull–sheltie mix. Answer the three questions they ask you wisely, and they will allow you to add your mattress to the heap. Answer them incorrectly, and they'll eat your face.

Your Soul
Recyclable.

PICKMAN'S CHICKEN FARM IS NOW CRUELTY-FREE

Zack Poitras

We would like to announce that Pickman's Chicken Farm is now a cruelty-free chicken farm.

Since our humble beginnings in 1994, Pickman's Chicken Farm has prided itself on providing free-range, organic chicken. We've never used antibiotics or hormones, and no pesticides ever touch our soil or feed. Now we are pleased to add "cruelty-free" to that list. Our chickens will not only be fed well, they will be treated well. No more inhumane slaughtering. No more senseless torture or deceit. No more efforts to debase the chickens and make them feel poor.

We're making improvements daily. The creaky rope bridge leading to the coop has been replaced with a ramp. In the past we would have greased the ramp to watch chickens fall on their dumb faces. Today? No grease. The pit of spikes under the bridge has been covered with a large board.

In the coop, the trapdoors situated over a vat of acid have been nailed shut. The thin glass panel separating the chickens from our fox pen—painted over. We've removed the hanging chains, guillotines, and rakes hidden beneath a thin layer of brush. The live video feed from our slaughterhouse has been disabled. When the chickens leave the coop, we no longer replace their nests with big rocks painted to look like nests.

We've put an end to the pranks. No more waking the chickens with a squirt of orange juice in the eyes, apologizing for our actions, wiping their eyes clean, and then, just as they are about to fall back asleep, squirting them in the eyes again. We also stopped gluing tiny beards to their beaks.

The chicken feed is now free of fake chicken eyeballs and little pebbles.

Chickens shall no longer be dangled from high places nor lashed to our feet prior to mashing grapes for our Pickman's Vineyard Signature Merlot. How this new rule will affect the wine's unique palate, we've yet to discover. But it's a risk our lawyers say we must take.

In the old days, we used to pluck a chicken down to one feather a couple weeks before killing it, just so its chicken friends could see what a ding-dong it is. That's over now.

We'll no longer put a chicken in a maze and slaughter it as a reward for solving the maze. And no more surprise firing squads, where we'd make chickens execute another chicken by shoving a wing in the trigger hole and tickling its belly. (We are currently researching how to kill chickens humanely and will follow suit.)

The decision to become a cruelty-free chicken farm was not easy. After all, chickens are lazy, stupid creatures that naturally deserve creative sadism and excessive poking. Humiliated chickens, especially the ones covered in maple syrup and rainbow sprinkles, evoke the purest form of human laughter, and there's no telling us different.

Unfortunately, our unbridled joy at chicken hazing started to negatively affect our business, and change became our only option. There had been complaints from the parents of children who visited the farm on a class field trip, no doubt a result of our encouraging each child to find a chicken to punch in the back of the head. A few grocery stores also took up issue after a few pounds of chicken gizzards showed up black from the chickens' forced addiction to cigarettes.

If only because we have to, we nevertheless embrace our new philosophy toward chicken treatment and are proud to join an elite class of farming. If you'd like to see Pickman's Chicken Farm's already substantial improvements, we invite you to stop by anytime. I recommend paying us a visit this Friday, when we'll be firing goats out of a hydraulic cannon into a big lake.

CREATE YOUR OWN THOMAS FRIEDMAN OP-ED COLUMN

Michael Ward

DISORDER AND DREAMS IN [COUNTRY IN THE NEWS]

Last week's events in [country in the news] were truly historic, although we may not know for years or even decades what their final meaning is. What's important, however, is that we focus on what these events mean [on the ground / in the street / to the citizens themselves]. The [media / current administration] seems too caught up in [worrying about / dissecting / spinning] the macro-level situation to pay attention to the important effects on daily life. Just call it missing the [desert for the sand / fields for the wheat / battle for the bullets].

When thinking about the recent turmoil, it's important to remember three things: One, people don't behave like [computer programs / billiard balls / migratory birds], so attempts to treat them as such inevitably look foolish. [Computer programs / Billiard balls / Migratory birds] never suddenly [blow themselves up / shift their course in order to fit with a predetermined set of beliefs / set up a black market for Western DVDs]. Two, [country in question] has spent decades [as a dictatorship closed to the world / being batted back and forth between colonial powers / torn by civil war and ethnic hatred], so a mindset of peace and stability will seem foreign and strange. And three, [hope / freedom / capitalism] is an extraordinarily powerful idea.

When I was in [country in question] last [week / month / August], I was amazed by the [people's basic desire for a stable life / level of Westernization for such a closed society / variety of the local cuisine], and that tells me two things. It tells me that the citizens of [country in question] have no shortage of [courage / potential entrepreneurs / root vegetables], and that is a good beginning to grow from. Second, it tells me that people in [country in question] are just like people anywhere else on this great globe of ours.

So what should we do about the chaos in [country in question]? Well, it's easier to start with what we should not do. We should not [ignore the problem and pretend it will go away / lob a handful of cruise missiles and hope that some explosions will snap (country in question)'s leaders to attention / let seemingly endless frustrations cause the people of (country in question) to doubt their chance at progress]. Beyond that, we need to be careful to nurture [the seeds of democratic ideals / the fragile foundations of peace / these first inklings of a moderate, modern society]. The opportunity is there, but I worry that the path to [peace / stability / moderation] is so [narrow / poorly marked / strewn with obstacles] that [country in question] will have to move down it very slowly.

Speaking with a local farmer on the last day of my recent visit, I asked him if there was any message that he wanted me to carry back home with me. He pondered for a second, and then smiled and said, "[Short phrase in indigenous language]," which is a local saying that means roughly, "[Every branch of the tree casts its own shadow / That tea is sweetest whose herbs have dried longest / A child knows his parents before the parents know their child]."

I don't know what [country in question] will be like a few years from now, but I do know that it will [probably look very different from the country we see now / remain true to its cultural heritage], even if it [remains true to its basic cultural heritage / looks very different from the country we see now]. I know this because, through all the disorder, the people still haven't lost sight of their dreams.

THE GAHHH! INSTITUTE

Lucas Klauss

Unemployment!

Health care!

The deficit!

Doesn't it all just make you want to scream?!

Us too! The Gahhh! Institute is a nonpartisan scream tank that promotes solutions to America's greatest challenges by SCREAMING REALLY LOUD!

Think tanks are obsolete! We would know, as we used to be one! Our quiet, respectful TV appearances and completely silent articles were *totally ineffective*! No matter how good our ideas were or how reasonably we explained them, Washington just kept getting more and more broken! After a string of emotional breakdowns and a steady diet of cable news, we realized the only way to get the government working again is TO SCREAM AT IT! That's the only way they'll G*DD@MN LISTEN TO YOU!

Your contributions to the Gahhh! Institute help keep us stocked with throat lozenges, herbal tea, and antidepressants! In return, we scream super-loud about the issues that matter to YOU!

IMMIGRATION!

ABORTION!

CLIMATE CHAAAAAAANGE!

Not just anybody with vocal cords can do what we do! Our extensive research into optimal screaming techniques gives us a HUGE advantage over AMATEUR POLITICAL SCREAMERS and even PEOPLE WITH BULLHORNS! Our Washington experience and SCHOLARLY APPEARANCES grant us access to rooms of power that large, unruly crowds have to STAND OUTSIDE OF and IMPOTENTLY CHANT AT! And our concise, insistent messaging ensures that the chattering classes LITERALLY CAN'T IGNORE US:

"Very loud!"—*The Washington Post*

"Obnoxious!"—*The New Republic*

"Please stop screaming at me!"—the guy who answers John Boehner's office phone

NO! We will NOT STOP SCREAMING until Congress and the president adopt our two-point plan:

1.   F*%KING FIX IT ALREADY!!!!!!!!!!!!!!!!!!!!!!!!!
2.   NOW!!!!!!!!!!!!!!!!!!!!!!!!

Many representatives and senators have already agreed to cosponsor the USA Fix Everything! bill in return for us NOT SCREAMING IN THEIR FACES! The USA Fix Everything! bill is our signature legislative proposal that will incorporate BIPARTISAN, RESEARCH-DRIVEN SOLUTIONS, which we will determine AT A LATER TIME! For now: Washington is finally paying attention to us! And admittedly, it feels PRETTY DAMN SATISFYING!

But we cannot rest our voices! Some in Congress have taken to WEARING EARPLUGS, and the president has gotten pretty good at HAVING HIS iPOD ON IN PUBLIC AND PRETENDING HE CAN'T HEAR US! Only with YOUR HELP will be able to hire our nation's GREATEST OPERA INSTRUCTORS to train our scream fellows! America ain't over until the PASTY WHITE BESPECTA-CLED GENTLEMAN sings!

Loudly,
Gary McKelly
Director of the Gahhh! Institute

EYEWITNESS NEWS WITH TOM DENARDO AND CHERYL CLAYBURN

Seth Reiss

. . . All those stories and more on tonight's *Eyewitness News*. Good evening, I'm Jarrod Palmer. Tom Denardo is off tonight.

Dana Gibson is also off tonight. Mark Batista is off tonight. Paula Winston is off tonight. James Hastings, Carol Montgomery, and Kevin Bosley are off tonight. David Lennox is off tonight. Molly Hutchins is off tonight. Amanda Carlson is either sick or on vacation, or she's off tonight. I think she's off tonight.

Adam Stapelton is off tonight. James McGrath is off tonight. Nancy Oliver is off tonight. Jason Nardozi is off tonight because this is the week he switches days with Pete Lipton. Pete Lipton, however, is sick. Trevor Einhorn is sick. Paul Granger is sick. I saw Paul the other day and he looked terrible. So did Lorraine Jacobs, who is not only sick but is also off tonight. She's not off tomorrow night, though, so we'll see what happens with that. Caroline Davis is currently filling in for Wes Shumar on the morning show. Wes Shumar is filling in for Heidi Witt on the afternoon broadcast, and Heidi Witt is off tonight.

Elizabeth Sherman is off tonight. Glenn Daniels is off tonight. Several people are currently looking for Chloe Hillman, but it doesn't matter because she's off tonight. Miranda and Tony are off tonight.

Naomi Martin is here but is refusing to go on air. The same goes for Mark Reynolds, Pauline Robinson, and Kurt, whose last name escapes me at the moment. Nobody knows where the hell Fran Irving is.

I'm now getting word that Fran Irving is, in fact, off tonight. Thanks, David. Sorry, Steve, you sound like David. David is off tonight.

We got a call this morning from Bob Clement. He said he is sick, but might be in later, whatever that means. Kelly Damico is off tonight because she just had a baby. Congratulations to Kelly and her husband, Aaron, who I've actually never met and have only seen in pictures. Zack Corkman is off tonight. Last time I saw Pam Greenberg she was in the hallway on her way here, so I don't know where she went. Steve Jepson might know. Steve is off tonight. Bill Statsky doesn't work here anymore. Jane Burton is off tonight, but no one's too upset about that. She's sort of a divisive figure around here.

Vince Basinger is the weatherman, and he's here. Sam Kemmis is also here, but he's just an old college friend of mine visiting for the weekend who wanted to see me do my thing. He is off tonight, but from a job that isn't this one. Trisha Ross is sick. The new guy, the one who sometimes fills in for Betty, that's me. I'm here. Betty is off tonight. Jenny Halfhill is currently on assignment, but works for another network, so why bring her up, you know? David Stanton is not here. He should be, but he's not.

Nathan Alford is off tonight. Harold Foreman is off tonight. Sarah Utley passed away last night in her sleep. She was forty-two. Ben Benzio is off tonight. His brother Stan Benzio is also off tonight. Kind of neat that two brothers are anchors at the same network, huh? Well, I think it's kind of neat. Bryce Fox is a kid I played Little League baseball with.

Bosley Mackelfresh is here, but Bosley Mackelfresh is a dog. The following pet animals, however, are sick: Clover, Mr. Oscar, and Flash. Jasper the Bloodhound is off tonight. Janet Ginsburg is sick. Rachel Koval is sick. Those last two are people, not animals. Natalie Maida is somebody I just made up. Lorrie Alster is real. She's off tonight.

Chuck Kellog is off tonight and would have been coming to you live. That would have been exciting. Chuck's the best. Erin Swink is not off tonight, but she's also not here. Personal day? Russell Crowe is off tonight. Yes, *that* Russell Crowe. Doug McConnell is off tonight. Yes, *that* Doug McConnell. Former Pittsburgh Pirates pitcher Doug Drabek is here, and will have the latest from City Hall after the weather. It's odd that he doesn't do sports. We all think that. Tara Morrow is off tonight.

And sitting next to me is Lynn Grimaldi, who is filling in for Cheryl Clayburn.

HOW MUCH I HAD TO MANIPULATE THE DATA TO MAKE IT SEEM LIKE THINGS WERE LOOKING UP

Ben Greenman

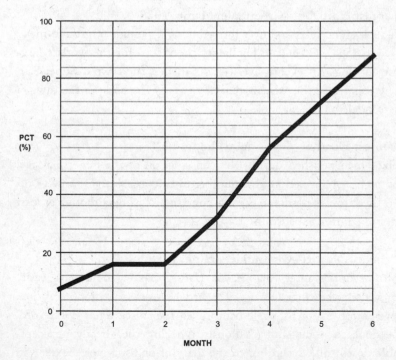

LITTLE-KNOWN FACTS FROM THE
GUINNESS BOOK OF WORLD RECORDS

Simon Rich

Largest Hot Dog—Greendale, Maine, 1928
It took eight years and over forty thousand pounds of ground meat, but in 1928, Greendale finally set the record for the world's largest hot dog. At seventy-five feet, six inches, the town's "Super Sausage" shattered the existing mark by twenty feet and put the town of Greendale on the map.

Vainest Deaths—Greendale, Maine, 1928
Sixty men perished during the construction of the Super Sausage. Some historians believe this number to be conservative. Most workers died from exposure to the hot dog's toxic casing, although at least four died from exhaustion.

Cruelest Mayor—Greendale, Maine, 1928
Most scholars agree that Mayor Harold Baxter could have easily prevented the tragedies of 1928 had he exercised proper caution. Even after his townspeople had broken the existing hot-dog record, he doubled night shifts, callously ignoring the already unacceptable death toll. According to the diary of one survivor, Baxter was

"obsessed with the Guinness record," to the point where it "blinded him to reason."

Harshest Irony—Greendale, Maine, 1929

When the U.S. stock market crashed, the town of Greendale was rocked by a devastating food shortage. Rioters stormed the Super Sausage in the hopes of divvying up its meat among their families. But Mayor Baxter had encased the sausage with bulletproof glass so it would "last until the end of the world."

Biggest Jelly Donut—Greendale, Maine, 1939

Somehow, Mayor Baxter held enough sway over the town of Greendale, Maine, that he was able to convince its citizens to build a second giant food item. The project took ten years. "I fear the mayor has gone mad," one survivor wrote. "But who can stand up to him?" In addition to causing an untold number of deaths, the project inflicted incalculable psychological damage on its workers, many of whom were denied basic human rights during the construction of the donut.

Longest Nails—Mayor Baxter, Greendale, Maine, 1941

Mayor Baxter's growing insanity became apparent in the early 1940s, when he stopped cutting his nails. Eventually, the National Guard removed him from office and placed him in a federal asylum, putting an end to one of the darkest chapters in American history. Today, the entire town of Greendale is a museum. The hot dog and donut have been destroyed and a peace tree stands in their place.

ONGOING ROADBLOCKS IN THE MONGOOSE-COBRA PEACE PROCESS

Bob Woodiwiss

1. Mongooses continue to demand that all negotiations take place in a cool, shaded crevice or underground burrow; this is necessary, they say, to prevent any overheating or excessive panting. The cobra delegation, however, citing their cold-bloodedness, flatly refuses to consider such cooler venues, arguing that temperatures below sixty-five degrees will make them lethargic, fuzzy-headed, and, "if past is prelude, a *buffet froid.*"

2. Cobras claim that, through no fault of their own, they are at an evolutionary disadvantage, a disadvantage they trace to the Oligocene epoch (33–23 million years ago). To restore a more historic primordial balance to cobra-mongoose relations, the reptiles suggest rolling back evolutionary mutations and adaptations on both sides to pre-Oligocene levels, in fact to the Cretaceous period (145–65 million years ago). Mongooses are quick to point out that in the Cretaceous period, mongooses did not exist.

3. Mongooses are pressuring cobras to provide them with low- or no-interest loans until they are able to develop sufficient alternative sources of food. Without such loans, mongooses say, they will have little choice but to return to the diet they've flour-

ished/relied on in the preceding eons. Cobras, citing their own loss of habitat and consequent recessionary economy, are appealing to leaders of several thriving local and worldwide orders and suborders for assistance, but, given the commonly held perception that snakes are highly slithery and untrustworthy, prospects for attracting potential lenders are generally seen as poor.

4. Cobras insist that mongooses aid in the recovery and return of all remains of reptilian combatants killed in action over the course of hostilities. In response, mongooses have agreed to cooperate, but only in the recovery of *discarded* remains, not, as stipulated by the cobras, *digested* remains.

5. Under pressure from an increasingly nervous population, mongooses are calling for the closure and dismantling of all training camps involved with instructing young cobras on how to become spitting cobras. Spitting cobras, with their ability to spray a lethal dose of venom into the eyes of a mongoose instead of using the traditional method of ineffectually biting the mammal's thick coat, pose a growing threat to mongooses and have been denounced as "radical venomists" by many predator-rights organizations. For their part, biting cobras officially condemn the use of venom delivered by expectoration and deny the existence of any such training camps, though they also concede cobras occupy a far-ranging habitat that is difficult to fully surveil.

6. The parties are at an impasse on the establishment of a so-called depredatorized zone (DPZ), a neutral strip of land on the mongoose-cobra frontier where all aggressive behaviors, postures, and scents are strictly forbidden. Cobras, while favoring the zone in principle, claim their aggression is instinctive, not voluntary, and should be exempted; mongooses make an identical assertion but add that they made it first, and therefore *they* should be exempted. The reptiles categorically deny the mammals' primacy claim, and separate negotiations to determine "ownership" (but not viability) of the proposed exemption are currently under discussion.

7. Mongooses are stipulating that all classified cobra neurotoxin formulae be turned over to mongoose scientists so that antidotes may be synthesized. Cobras contend that sharing such information would leave them without a realistic deterrent. Neither side acknowledges the utter preposterousness of mongoose scientists.

THE GIRLS OF *THE HILLS* VISIT AFGHANISTAN

Wendy Molyneux

{LAUREN, AUDRINA, and WHITNEY walk along a desert highway, escorted by U.S. soldiers.}

AUDRINA: Oh my God. This is sad.

LAUREN: It is sad.

WHITNEY: It's sad.

AUDRINA: It's so sad.

LAUREN: So sad.

{Long pause.}

LAUREN: When you think about it, it's sad.

{LAUREN's Sidekick beeps.}

WHITNEY: Who's texting you?

AUDRINA: Is it Brody?

LAUREN: Yeah.

AUDRINA: Oh my God, he loves you.

WHITNEY: Oh my God, that soldier looks like he's, like, eighteen.

LAUREN: He does not love me. We're friends.

WHITNEY: He's younger than us.

AUDRINA: Brody is not younger than us! You're so crazy, Whitney.

WHITNEY: Wow, he's younger than us and he's over here without his parents, going out on patrol every day with no idea whether he'll come back.

LAUREN: Oh my God!

AUDRINA: What?

LAUREN: Brody saw Spencer and Heidi last night at Opera. And Spencer danced with another girl.

AUDRINA: Oh my God! That's crazy.

WHITNEY: It is crazy. Why do you think we send off to war our youngest and most vulnerable, those who could stay to build our nation, when time and again these wars prove themselves to be fools' errands? It has to be more than the economic need to support the military-industrial complex. It seems like there's also a need to restore the heroic, youthful face of post–World War II America with a victory abroad, yet we ensure that that symbolic face is corrupted and annihilated by choosing conflicts that can only controvert that image.

[*LAUREN's Sidekick beeps again.*}

LAUREN: No way!

WHITNEY: You disagree? Look at that soldier.

LAUREN: Heidi just texted me that she and Spencer broke up!

AUDRINA: No!

LAUREN: This is huge.

WHITNEY: I fucking hate you guys.

{A shot rings out. WHITNEY drops out of frame.}

AUDRINA: I want, like, a juice or something.

LAUREN: Brody does kind of love me, huh?

AUDRINA: Yeah.

DAVID BROOKS ALSO EATS CEREAL

John Warner

There's been a lot of talk about tea this political season, but I want to discuss something different as it relates to breakfast: cereal.

I believe that there are two types of people in the world: those who like to look into their bowl at a sea of desiccated marshmallows, and those who prefer an unsweetened alternative made from whole-grain oats. I call them the Lucky Charmers and the Cheerioians.

Lucky Charmers hold their spoons overhand-style and make slurping noises as they eat. Sometimes, they even try to pluck the marshmallows out with their fingers because the marshmallows bob up and down in the milk, which makes it very hard to get at them with just a spoon. Sometimes, they don't even pour the cereal into a bowl, and eat right out of the box.

Cheerioians, on the other hand, often eat their cereal entirely unadorned, unless they choose to top it with sliced bananas or strawberries. They hold their spoons correctly and make love to their spouses three times a month. They are lured by the boxes that promise lower cholesterol or healthier colons. They often drink orange juice from a glass or coffee out of a mug. Maybe they work in insurance or as columnists for major metropolitan papers. They are the America that exists mostly in my own head.

Lucky Charmers prefer apple juice and drink out of a sippy cup.

On occasion, they will even fling their cereal bowls over their heads and shriek, "Wheeeeeeeee!" They are free spenders, preferring a windup toy that will break within the day to a money-saving coupon in the bottom of the box. They watch *SpongeBob*, during which they giggle.

Sometimes, a Cheerioian will abandon cereal altogether and grab a bagel as they run out the door. Increasingly often, the Cheerioian won't even have time for breakfast. A Cheerioian who has skipped breakfast is nothing to trifle with.

There was a time in all of our lives when we were Lucky Charmers, when we could ignore the consequences of a morning sucrose bomb on our metabolism, our dental health, our fight against Islamic terrorism, our budget deficits, and governmental debt. But now, post-9/11, post-boom, we find ourselves heading into a more serious and sober world, a world where we can no longer accept the empty promises of artificially sweetened candy passing itself off as a healthy breakfast. The Lucky Charmers have fallen prey to a sham, a mirage, a magically delicious but dangerous world coming out of the mouths of leprechauns. Green clovers and yellow moons are not going to turn our wayward republic in the right direction. Purple horseshoes, either.

Though we could use a few more pots of gold.

In the past I have also been critical of Cheerioians, not because I have actual convictions or a consistent worldview, but because I have a pathological need to seem reasonable.

But we can't afford to ignore this menace any longer. Let's get together and do something vague and platitudinous for which I can't be held personally accountable.

A STRAW POLL OF ISSUES ON VOTERS' MINDS FOR THIS UPCOMING ELECTION, BASED ONLY ON THE CONVERSATION INITIATIONS OF THE MOROSE SECURITY GUARD WHO SITS IN THE LOBBY OF THE BUILDING WHERE I WORK

Ryan Haney

I need a new job.

I've been sick for so long.

Is that sweater warm?

Where did you get that lunch?

All I hear is sirens all day. Someone's probably dead.

Is that sweater wool?

You don't have to wear a hat when it's cold out if you drink a lot.

They don't let me leave to get lunch.

No sweater today?

Every time I've tried leaving the building, it's started raining.

PHOTO OPS TO GAIN MORE THAN 50% OF THE ELECTORATE

David Hart

Playing speed chess with Willie Nelson while shotgunning a Coors

Scoring winning soccer goal with church youth group and high-fiving the Dalai Lama

Pie-eating contest with Betty White while lifting up a copy of the Torah

Holding a baby bald eagle and a kitten while standing next to *Baywatch*-era Pam Anderson

Jet Skiing with Hulk Hogan and Noam Chomsky or snowboarding with Justin Bieber and Jesse Ventura

Dunking a basketball over Vladimir Putin's head while eating a Hot Pocket

At Mount Rushmore, jumping a motorcycle over fifteen exploding school buses while holding a flag reading "Putting Americans Back to Work"

Breaking through a banner reading "Tax Reform Now!" while cannonballing into a pool of red, white, and blue Jell-O

Onstage with AC/DC, putting Mahmoud Ahmadinejad in a head-lock with one arm, Goldman Sachs CEO Lloyd Blankfein with the other

At Graceland, karate-chopping three boards painted with the words "Corruption," "Government," and "Terrorism," respectively

Jumping off the top rope at WrestleMania while holding an Uzi, flashing a peace sign, and wearing a cape labeled "Freedom"

DANCE DANCE REVOLUTION

Matthew Bonnano

Bolero
Fandango
Proletarian

Salsa
Samba
Bolshevik

Waltz
Quickstep
American

Jig
Lindy Hop
Industrial

Merengue
Swing
Social

Foxtrot
Mazurka
Bloodless Coup

ACTUAL SUBJECT LINES OF E-MAILS I'VE RECEIVED FROM BARACK OBAMA'S CAMPAIGN THAT SOUND LIKE HE'S ASKING ME OUT AND THEN BREAKING UP WITH ME

Sarah Walker

What are you doing this Tuesday?
Sarah, can we meet for dinner?
How this dinner thing works
Yes or no, Sarah?
I will not take no for an answer
Saved seats
How about a T-shirt?
If I don't call you
Very soon
Frustrated
It's officially over
Fixing what's broken

FRAGMENTS FROM *SANTORUM!*
THE MUSICAL

Ben Greenman

Premiere: October 12, 2012

Performances: 3

Note: *Rick Santorum himself produced this musical, which he had envisioned as a musical spectacular but which became, over the course of workshopping, a one-man endeavor. Santorum insisted that the show premiere on October 12, which is Kirk Cameron's birthday, and that it close on October 14, which is Roger Moore's birthday. "I think of myself as a combination of those two men," he said, assuming there were reporters around to hear his remark. There weren't. Santorum was played by Eugene Tetescomesco, a young actor and dancer who later earned fame as the star of the hour-long drama* Blammo! *on CBS.*

———

{An empty room. It is quiet and peaceful. Suddenly a brick on the wall pops out and tumbles to the floor. A second brick follows. When a half-dozen are gone, a face appears at the hole: RICK SANTORUM's face.}

RICK SANTORUM

Appearing here at this brick wall

Is a kind of birth
I'm crowning, you could say
So give me a wide berth
Sure: I rhymed two homonyms
It's permitted in this game.
(It doesn't mean "gay words," you know
Just two words that sound the same.)
And so I'm crowning, being born
I'm happening before your eyes
My star fell in Pennsylvania
But now my star begins to rise
I'm crowning like a president
Instead of crowning like a king
I'm coming into view, you see,
I'm coming into view to sing.

{RICK SANTORUM clears his throat. He opens his mouth and a single high note emerges, a wordless stream of sound. At first it is arresting, then annoying, then monotonous, and at length it is not noticed anymore. When RICK SANTORUM realizes that no one is listening, he stops singing and makes a case for himself.}

RICK SANTORUM

I am singing! I am Rick!
My voice is ringing out. The trick
To being me is to remain
On point, on message, never waver.
By that strategy I will become
The GOP's undaunted savior.

{No one is listening. RICK SANTORUM looks around and then converts his embarrassment into purpose. He does so naturally, as if he has done it before.}

RICK SANTORUM

No more singing for me now.
I've got more to do anyhow.
I must go now and hector Mitt
About the ongoing perception
That he panders to the electorate
And also is procontraception
And also I will go fight Newt
He's always up for a dispute
At any time, in any forum
And so am I. I'm Rick Santorum.

*{The bricks lift off the floor and replace themselves in the wall, one by one.
When the wall is bricked back up, RICK SANTORUM can be heard faintly
from behind the wall.}*

RICK SANTORUM

I was wrong to stop singing
Now I can't move this brick
I'm going down swinging
I'm Rick! I'm Rick!

{Fade to black, then bring the lights back up to a moderate gray.}

SPREADING THE GOOD WORD:
A MISSIONARY'S GUIDE

Wendy Molyneux

Let's face it. Not everybody is ready to hear the word of the Lord. Many people have excuses about why they aren't ready to take Jesus into their hearts, such as: "How can I believe in God when the world is filled with pain?" or "I'm a Jew." So how do you spread the word of the Messiah to everybody? Read below to find the group you're targeting, memorize the script, then get out there and sell!

Teenagers

TROUBLED TEEN: Man, Jesus is boring. I'd rather ride my BMX bicycle, smoke reefer, and get handjobs.

MISSIONARY: Whoa, there! You think Jesus is boring?! Well, check this out: one time Jesus was chilling at this party, when . . . what? Aw, hell no. The guy throwing the party didn't buy enough wine. Everybody was about to leave, when, out of nowhere, Jesus made a whole grip of wine, and some tasty-ass snacks. Having a guy around who can create a keg out of thin air would be pretty helpful to somebody who can't buy beer, am I right, bro?

TROUBLED TEEN: I never knew Jesus liked to party.

MISSIONARY: Word. (Of the Lord!)

Feminists

FEMINIST: Jesus is the figurehead of a patriarchal religion that teaches women that they are second to men in all things.

MISSIONARY: You're really pretty.

FEMINIST: What? Really?

MISSIONARY: Yeah, I mean, it's not an obvious kind of prettiness— it's subtler. You look a little like Marisa Tomei.

FEMINIST: (*sobs*) Nobody has ever said that to me before. That's why I'm so angry.

MISSIONARY: I bet you've had some pretty bad experiences with men. But I'd like to give you a good one. What are you doing on Friday?

FEMINIST: I was going to go to a Take Back the Night march, but . . .

MISSIONARY: . . . you'd rather go to Applebee's and get to know me better? You don't mind if I bring my wingman, do you? His name is Our Lord.

Robots

ANDROID: The Bible does not mention artificial intelligence.

MISSIONARY: Look, HelpBot 6-900, I'm not supposed to tell you this, but there was a whole bunch of stuff in the Bible about robots. It got cut out. It says so in *The Da Vinci Code.*

ANDROID: Are you sure?

MISSIONARY: How do you think people did all that crazy stuff: walking on water, killing giants, forgiving their families? Normal humans can't do that stuff. Those were robots.

ANDROID: I knew that humans were lying to me. Must kill all humans. Must kill.

Missionary: Oops.

Democrats

DEMOCRAT: Actually, I'm already a Christian. I go to First Presbyterian.

MISSIONARY: I don't get it.

DEMOCRAT: I know.

THE 700 CLUB DOES WEATHER

Alex Kane

Good morning, folks. This is Ricky Rogers, your morning weatherman. Let's take a look at the map.

Now, we can see patches of precipitation around the Midwest. That should pass by midafternoon. Taking a look over the northwestern states, however, there will be some serious thunderstorms lasting all into tonight, and we can pretty much guess that those are tears the angels are shedding because it is still legal for a woman to end the life of her unborn child.

Hurricane season is now in effect, and we all remember what happened last year. This year may be even worse due to an increase in the frequency of evil deeds. Blame San Francisco. So, if you live near the Gulf Coast, invest in floatation devices and Bibles.

It is hot, hot, hot today in New York City, which should give all the Jews there a bit of a sneak preview.

Las Vegas, Nevada, has been suffering a bit of a drought lately, but we've got some good news for you folks: thirty-nine to forty-one consecutive days and nights of rain coming soon. You can "bet" on it!

Weather across Georgia will be perfect. Absolutely perfect. You know why.

In your city today, it's looking like about an eighty percent chance of hail and harsh winds, but you could probably get that down to fifty percent if you tossed out all of your dirty magazines and concentrated on keeping homosexuals from getting married.

That's it for me. I'll be back on with weather updates throughout the morning, unless the Day of Judgment comes, in which case I will be called upon to live in eternal peace in our Father's heavenly kingdom.

Keep it real.

THE FIRST AMERICAN BIDDING WAR

Susan Schorn

29 September, 1776

Dear Mistress Ross,

Our deepest thanks and gratitude to you for the wondrous flag of diverse stripes & stars, which we received this Thursday last from your esteemed shoppe. Truly the Second Continental Congress is most pleased and astonished by its craft, detail, and many Instances of fine American workmanship. Your Substitution of five-pointed stars for the traditional six-cornered style, in especial, represents an inspired Break with the tyranny of old-world aesthetic convention, and is a fitting attribute for this first flag of our new nation.

Alas, tho' this flag itself is most excellent in every regard, and a stirring symbol of our cause, yet we must regretfully decline to accept your accompanying bid, viz., to supply like flag of matching design and size, at the price of 1/3 dollar a piece, for the various branches of the newly formed Continental Army. Tho' all of us here assembled are agreed that this is a fair and reasonable Valuation, given the Quality of the wares in question, yet the Congress has received this very week, a competing bid for similar flags, to be speedily manufactured on the distant islands called Cayman, and sent aboard fast merchant ships, to American shores, all for the cost of a mere 1/5 dollar a piece.

While these tropically sourced flags will doubtless be of somewhat inferior make, being necessarily composed of foreign-grown cotton, and stitched by the less-skilled and perhaps ill-nourished hands of foreign women and children, yet Congress cannot escape the conclusion, that the lower price, coupled with the speed and convenience of delivery (for which we are assured there shall be no additional Charge appended), compels us to favor the foreign manufacturer with our custom. And besides, as Mr. Franklin has most wittily pointed out, workmanship may be of less concern in a flag that is destined to be shot to pieces by British cannon fire, than it is in a lady's petticoats, which must withstand more perilous assaults.

Howsoever, should you be desirous of bidding on future military contracts from a more advantageous footing, I implore you to consider moving your upholstery shoppe to one of those several Islands, such as Turks & Caicos, where cheap labor is to be had, free of the stranglehold of the apprenticeship system. The Congress, aware of its financial duty to the people it represents, finds these islands an ideal partner in commerce, as the merchants there are able to equip our troops at very low cost to our fledgling nation's Treasury.

Even now, several members of our Congress are themselves engaged in moving their own manufactories (some of which, by the most astounding coincidence, produce goods required by the Army) to these same regions. Doubtless you too would find the costs of producing your wares lower if you followed their prudent example. The pirates and fever-inducing miasmas native to the islands are, their denizens assure us, mere trifling annoyances and more than compensated for by the considerable tax advantages they offer to industry.

For it must be observed, that the very reason of our uprising against the British crown, and its vexatious, illegal taxes, is our desire to retain more of that wealth, which God is pleased to allow us to earn, by our own hard work, or that of our Children, indentured servants, or slaves. Indeed, what is the object of revolution, if not to throw off the outrageous yoke of taxation unnaturally imposed by the crown, so that we may freely and cheerfully evade the taxes imposed by our own, sovereign Laws?

"No Taxation without Representation!" as the Reverend Mayhew has said, to which Mr. Franklin adds, "And even then, you shall have to catch us first!" He is exceedingly droll, is Mr. Franklin, and keeps all the members of this Congress positively rolling with laughter.

I close with a humble reminder, that an army cannot march without an inspiring and competitively priced flag to follow, and care must likewise be duly taken that a nation have a worthy leader at its head. Never was such executive office won without sufficient funds for the campaign and promotion of the candidate, however worthy. If your shoppe should wish to make a small donation, to the coffers of the Washington for President Committee, our nation would no doubt repay you many times over in Gratitude. Those staunch friends of our Republic, who give 500 dollars or more, earn the special status of "Patriot," and receive a sterling silver lapel pin, in the form of an eagle.

Yours in the cause of liberty and freedom,
Geo. Washington, Maj. General

THE FRONT PORCH CAMPAIGN, 1880

Chris White

Gentlemen, welcome! Our Union stands today on the ramparts of a fortress built from our triumphs.

And upon my lawn. Look, if you could stay inside the cordons, it would make Lucretia so happy. We just resodded, and you know how women are. Thank you.

Okay. Right. Cordons, my fellow citizens, are not to be feared or loathed, but embraced. For as we stare down from the mighty fortress into the Valley of Prosperity into which we must venture, the cordons of law and liberty delineate a path free from peril, a path unspoiled by discarded chicken wings.

I'm looking at you, sir, in the straw hat. Don't act like you don't know what I'm talking about. I was staring right at you when you dropped it. It's free food! And the garbage can is four feet away. Four damn feet. You can spit farther than that. I saw you do so, onto my son's pet dog. So why don't you go take care of that.

Yes, I'm going to wait.

Was that so hard?

But you see now the great struggle of this experiment, this self-government which we hold so dear. We must be eternally vigilant against the straw hats of this world, as we learned in the great conflict that so rent our nation's core, and sweet Christ, who defecated in the rosebush? Do you think this is funny? There are like five outhouses right there! My kids play on this lawn. I don't want to think that they're running around with you cads dangling your privates out in broad daylight. Heavens forfend!

Are you even listening? I have about fifteen minutes here on civil service reform that we really need to get through. The great machinery of democracy cannot function with the gears so clogged by insidious clients of patronage.

Nor can we ignore the problem of brass bands ruining our lives. You, trombonists! Please go away! No one invited you here. Don't give them any money, I beg you. They play all hours of the night, and we are sorely taxed. Lucretia cries when she hears a march anymore. She CRIES. Did someone drop another chicken wing? I swear to God I will drop out of this race. Is that what you want? Because that's what I'm going to do.

To conclude, as I fire this shotgun into the air, I assure you it is loaded not with the rock salt of temerity, but in fact with the shells of righteous indignation. Our nation will sail steadfast and true into the Harbor of Opportunity, but only after you bastards get off my lawn. Vote Garfield.

PERHAPS NOW YOU WISH YOU HAD PAID CLOSER ATTENTION TO YOUR JUDICIAL CANDIDATES FOR COUNTY CIRCUIT COURT!

Mike Lacher

Citizens of Cook County, Illinois, by now you have all come to accept your enslavement to me, Overlord Phaxon, twenty-third ruler of the Worm People of the Horsehead Nebula. But perhaps you are still wondering how you suddenly ended up in such total subjugation to a race of spacefaring, marrow-drinking, superintelligent giant worms? Simple, my slaves, you failed to closely evaluate your judicial candidates for county circuit court!

A few months ago, some of you walked into your local polling places with the intention of actively participating in your "democracy." You voted for the senator you felt strongly about and against the pieces of social legislation you found objectionable. And then, my dear marrow factories, you laid eyes upon the lengthy list of county circuit judges. Perhaps you thought you knew what you were doing, or perhaps you simply didn't want to leave them blank out of fear of seeming apathetic. So you quickly voted for candidates who fit your party and seemed to have recognizable names. But those, my little flesh pods, were all worm people in disguise!

Take, for example, "Robert O'Brien, Democrat." Certainly seemed like the name of a decent, Irish, Democratic judicial candidate. But, in fact, each vote for "Robert O'Brien, Democrat" was a vote for my spawnling, Gimlor—the very same worm person who controls all of your spinal inhibitors! And what of "Allen Ackley, Democrat?" Many of you voted for him because his name was listed first on the ballot. But, in fact, it was our Chief of Nutrients, Galthax!

And "Bradley Kennedy, Democrat?" Not related to the Kennedys! Merely a deceptive and alluring pseudonym for Mulsh, our Spore Collector!

Yes, now perhaps as you sit there in your mucous pod, your marrow slowly excreting through your bones and out your nose, you begin to realize how your great ordeal came to be. You voted based on nothing but irrational instincts. And soon the courts were filled with nothing but disguised worm people, and quickly we began to assume power, one county ordinance at a time. As we processed eviction orders, small claims, and child custody hearings, our intake orifices could almost taste your sweet marrow.

Soon the way was paved, our forces landed, and we ripped off our human masks. Your pathetic armed forces attempted to stop our queen from spraying her breeding syrup into your water, but it was too late! We already had control of your county circuit courts. All that was left to do was gather you into our extraction chambers, implant your spinal inhibitors, and wait for the marrow to begin flowing.

Fear not, my little blood farms, you are only the beginning. We are in other counties, circulating petitions and disguising our bile chutes while we secure funding for bus signs and make speeches for party backing. Soon we will control all the county circuit courts. And then it is only a matter of time before we control the deputy sheriffs, the county comptrollers, and the world!

ORDINARY CIRCLE OR PIE CHART?

Ben Greenman

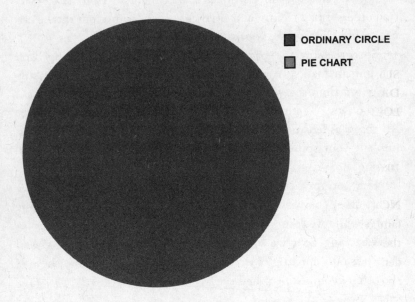

■ ORDINARY CIRCLE

■ PIE CHART

THIS IS A REELECTION CAMPAIGN STOP, NOT A LABOR DAY WEEKEND BEACH VACATION

Ryan Haney

NOTICE TO ALL STAFFERS
SUBJECT: PRESIDENT'S REELECTION CAMPAIGN ITINERARY
DATE: SEPTEMBER 1, 2012
LOCATION: CAPE COD, MASSACHUSETTS

10:00 AM - BREAKFAST / SANDI'S DINER / CHATHAM, MA

NOTES: The president will visit Sandi's to sample their "Cape-famous" pancakes. The St. Catherine's Knights of Columbus frequent the diner after their Saturday-morning meetings, giving the president an opportunity to get in touch with Chatham's baby boomers on the issues affecting an entire generation of Americans. The size of Sandi's Buttermilk Lumberjack Stack will afford the president plenty of time to listen in as the tables around him discuss the state of Medicare and financing their retirement.

12:30 PM - BEACH VISIT / LIGHTHOUSE BEACH / CHATHAM, MA

NOTES: The president will roll up his sleeves and strap on his sandals to get a firsthand look at the town's tourism industry, which has been hit hard by a downturned economy. Beaches have seen fewer and fewer visitors this year, so after a quick dip in the ocean and a light nap, the president will try to get an idea of the challenges facing our nation's seasonally employed while purchasing a paddleball set from Rob Norwich, owner and operator of Chatham Surf, Sand, and Sport.

Before departure, the president will demonstrate his continued commitment to his K–12 Reading Challenge by dragging his beach chair down to the water's edge and polishing off the last few chapters of *The Hunger Games*.

2:00 PM - SHOPPING / DENNISPORT CRANBERRY ARTS AND CRAFTS FESTIVAL / DENNISPORT, MA

NOTES: The president will take time to acknowledge small companies like Just in the Knit of Time and Scents and Sensibility that carry on this country's long and proud manufacturing tradition. While so many businesses continue to outsource factory jobs to foreign competitors, the microwaveable-neck-pillow, driftwood-key-rack, and dried-flower-shadowbox industries are showcasing American craftsmanship and providing gainful employment right here at home.

The president will also encourage consumers across the country to help stimulate the economy with their spending this holiday season by getting some early Christmas shopping out of the way and purchasing a set of sand-dollar drink coasters for the First Lady's sister.

4:15 PM - PARASAILING / DENNIS WATER WINGS / EAST DENNIS, MA

NOTES: Strapped into a parachute and towed behind a boat with its twin outboard motors at full throttle, the president will have a bird's-eye view of the erosion of seaside properties caused by a particularly strong hurricane season. Pending the availability of a properly fitting harness, Don Torrington, Dennis resident who lost his home during a recent storm, has been invited to share his experience while riding "tandem" with the president. The president will introduce his new FEMA assistance initiatives directly after his "Wonder Woman's Invisible Jetplane" photo opportunity.

7:00 PM - LASER TAG / NIGHT HAWK'S LAZER ADVENTURE / HARWICH, MA

NOTES: The dim, disorienting, close-quarters design of Night Hawk's Lazer Adventure will give the president a true approximation of the urban warfare conditions our armed forces are currently facing in the Middle East. With the aid of his top military advisors, the president will go through a number of simulations, including squad-based maneuvering tactics, free-for-all, and "Rockin' Fog and Strobe." Post-match, the president will sit down with his advisors to discuss troop withdrawal strategies over the pepperoni pizza that comes free with a purchase of five or more games.

LAURA WINGFIELD FROM *THE GLASS MENAGERIE* ON THE 2012 REPUBLICAN PRESIDENTIAL CANDIDATES

Kate Hahn

They're all so fragile. But each is beautiful in his or her own way. Some people say you can see right through them and that there's nothing to them at all. But that couldn't be more wrong! When the light hits them you realize that each and every one of them has the ability to make a rainbow. You just have to choose which rainbow you want.

Do you think I'm silly, Jim? It was so good of you to come over to watch the presidential primary debate. We've barely seen each other since high school. I'm sorry the power went out. It's these rolling blackouts due to deferred maintenance on the country's power grid.

I just hope the candidates aren't in the dark! They so love being well lit. You can just tell by looking at them. It warms them and makes their exquisitely carved forms sparkle so. I'm sure the TV will come back on any minute now, but for the moment we can enjoy the candles.

To be honest, I don't mind taking a little pause from watching. The reporters are so rough with the candidates I'm half afraid they'll break them. They ask them too many hard questions and try to pin them down, which could make them shatter into a million pieces. Why would anyone want to do that to such delicate things? The media can be so cruel. Americans don't want that. We're nice. Most reporters have a liberal bias—at least that's what Mother says. (*A peal of girlish laughter is heard from the kitchen.*)

Tom argues with her about that, of course. Remember when he stormed out of the apartment last month? It tickles me to think of it. He came back home three days later saying he was never going to get the life experience he needs to be a real writer. But he's already found some work through Craigslist, copyediting training manuals for call centers in India! I tell him the candidates will make everything better, but he just stares off into space. He says he feels responsible for me, being that so many people are on unemployment and I don't even have job training.

That last part I feel so guilty about. There's something I should confess to him, but I can't. I hope you don't mind if I unburden myself to you. The real reason I stopped going to Rubicam's Business College—well, it wasn't because I had social anxiety, like everyone thought. The student loans were just too much of a burden. The fifty dollars Mother gave me for class wasn't enough to buy a textbook! I couldn't bear to tell her, so I just donated the money to one of the candidates instead.

Which one? My favorite is the one with the single horn. It's different from the rest. All the others have two.

Tom would be so mad if he knew what I'd done. He says the candidates are out of touch with regular Americans. But I don't mind that they have to be kept on a little shelf and polished and cared for. They're special, after all. It's dangerous for them without their security guards and media-relations people. If you just breathe on

them, they'll break. And who would want that? To even think it is
un-American.

The power will come back on any minute now, Jim. I know it will,
and then I'll blow out these candles.

NO COUNTRY FOR ANYONE

John Warner

INT. DINER ON A DUSTY STRETCH OF DESOLATE ARROYO HUNDREDS OF MILES FROM THE NEAREST DECENT-SIZED TOWN—DAY

{A SHERIFF and his DEPUTY sit together while eating breakfast. Two eggs over easy, link sausage, toast—with a half-melted pat of butter in the middle—and hash browns sit untouched on the SHERIFF's plate. The DEPUTY shovels oatmeal into his mouth. The SHERIFF leafs through the paper.}

SHERIFF: (*Sighing from the deepest marrow of his bones.*) Says here there's gon' be an election.

DEPUTY: (*Mouth full of oatmeal.*) Seems I heard somethin' 'bout that.

SHERIFF: Yep?

DEPUTY: Yep.

SHERIFF: (*Continuing to turn the newspaper pages.*) You know what I reckon?

DEPUTY: No, sir. I surely don't.

SHERIFF: I reckon it don't matter who wins.

DEPUTY: Sheriff?

SHERIFF: I'm sayin' it don't matter who wins.

DEPUTY: Why you sayin' that, Sheriff?

SHERIFF: (*Turning the page in the paper.*) Says here there's a man in West Gulch . . .

DEPUTY: I got a cousin down in West Gulch.

SHERIFF: Well, this man in West Gulch, he took . . .

DEPUTY: Second cousin, actually. Mom's side. Lost an arm in a backhoe accident . . .

SHERIFF: (*Slightly exasperated.*) Anyway . . . this West Gulch man. Seems like while he was eating dinner he got some kind of compulsion to go pick up his television and smash it over his wife's head.

DEPUTY: You sayin' that a man killed his wife with his television?

SHERIFF: (*Slightly more exasperated.*) Nope. I'm sayin' a man smashed his wife over the head with his television. She weren't dead afterwards, just knocked out, so after that this West Gulch man took his wife over his shoulder and carried her out back and dug a hole and put her into the hole up to her neck. She was still wearing that television like some kind of hat, and then he poured some Karo syrup over the top and just let the ants have at her. Doesn't say nothin' here about her screamin', but I reckon there was some screamin'. At least if'n she woke up.

DEPUTY: (*Pushing oatmeal away.*) I reckon.

SHERIFF: After a while, seems that the vultures found her, started in those lazy circles overhead, bearing down on this woman with the television smashed over her head, buried in the hole and eaten at by the ants, and the neighbors noticed, thinkin' that maybe someone's cow got caught in the razor wire and died, so they went to take a look and saw the woman in the hole, with the television on her head and the ants, and they called the sheriff down there, Jim Fred . . .

DEPUTY: I know the man.

SHERIFF: (*Fully exasperated.*) Shut the fuck up, son. I'm telling a story that's got a real theme to it here.

DEPUTY: Sorry, Sheriff.

SHERIFF: So Jim Fred pulls up to the house and he can smell the woman, so he doesn't really need to go look, but he does anyway— and that's something he's going to regret, I can tell you; you don't forget something like that; something like that sticks with you— and then he goes into the man's house and finds the man sittin' in his chair, just staring at the space where that television used to be, and Jim Fred asks him what he has to say about his wife, buried outside in that hole with the television on her head, and the ants and now the vultures, and you know what the man says?

DEPUTY: No, Sheriff. I sure don't.

SHERIFF: The man says, "That's my art." "That's my art," the man says. What do you think that means, son?

DEPUTY: I surely don't know, Sheriff.

SHERIFF: I guess I don't fully know, either, son, but something I do know is that in a world where a man will get up, smash a television over his wife's head, and then bury her in a hole and pour Karo syrup over her for the ants, it seems like there's a madness out there, a real madness, the kind of madness you just cain't get hold of, and when there's a real madness out there, I reckon it don't matter one way or another who the president is. What good's a president against somethin' like that?

DEPUTY: No good at all, I reckon.

SHERIFF: I reckon.

{A WAITRESS approaches the table carrying a coffee decanter in each hand. It is clear that she was once a beauty, perhaps a local pageant winner, where the prize was a semester's tuition at the state university, a ticket out, but after a year there, Mama got sick and the WAITRESS had to come back to take care of her and Daddy, and when Mama passed she went to work at the diner and never left, her former beauty slowly fading like the evening sun dipping below the horizon.}

WAITRESS: More coffee, Sheriff?

SHERIFF: (*Holding up his cup for the pour.*) I reckon I better.

{Cut to: A vast panorama of the arroyo. Small bluffs in the distance lift toward the sky. Dust blows. Spikes of heat lightning dive for the ground.}

CANDIDATE: (*Voice-over.*) My name is [insert name here], and I reckon this is my message.

THE LATEST DEALS FROM LIVINGCAPITALIST

Pete Reynolds

$20 for $10 worth of groceries at Whole Foods

2 yoga classes for the price of 2.5

Freely contract among various competitors for teeth-whitening services

Pay the intersection of supply and demand for scuba lessons at Scuba! Scuba!

Save 30% on Invisible Hand manicures at Enlightenment Spa

Save 35% on manicures at Scuba! Scuba!

$2,000 to outsource your manufacturing to a country with 70% fewer child-labor laws

Deregulate yourself at Five Guys Burgers and Fries

Add 50% on Japanese cuisine at Tokyo House

Privatize your sidewalk for $499

Leave a briefcase full of cash in the foyer at 45 Wall Street

60% off collective bargaining rights

Free market

VOTER SEGMENTS TO WATCH THIS YEAR

Sloan Schang

Moderate concierges
Urban drum majors
Breakfast-for-dinner fans
MTV's *Real World* cast members (1992–1998)
Houseboat pioneers
Mall Santas under thirty-five
MTV's *Real World* cast members (1999–present)
Actual Tempur-Pedic bed owners
_____@hotmail.coms
Sunglasses-at-night types
People with mopeds
Nonsmoking ranch hands
Rationals
Irrationals
Bearded indecisives
Flautists

ACCUSATIONS LEVELED AT A DOLPHIN RUNNING FOR PRESIDENT

Eric Feezell

Never even left his pod
All squawk, no substance
Sea World sympathizer
Wet behind the ears
Flipper-flopper
Actually a wholphin

GOD TEXTS THE TEN COMMANDMENTS

Jamie Quatro

1. no1 b4 me. srsly.
2. dnt wrshp pix/idols
3. no omg's
4. no wrk on w/end (sat 4 now; mab sun 18r)
5. pos ok - ur m&d r cool
6. dnt kill ppl
7. :-X only w/ m8
8. dnt steal
9. dnt lie re: bf
10. dnt ogle ur bf's m8. or ox. or dnkey. myob.

M, pls rite on tabs & giv 2 ppl.

ttyl, YHWH.

ps. wwjd?

NEW FEARS FOR THE TWENTY-FIRST CENTURY

Hannah Tepper

1. Fear of the Internet.
2. Fear of not being on the Internet.

FRAGMENTS FROM *STRONG GOVERNMENT! THE MUSICAL*

Ben Greenman

Premiere: November 5, 2012
Performances: 1
Note: *The night before the 2012 presidential election, this musical was staged simultaneously at fifty different polling places across the nation. The show's fill-in-the-blanks aspect, which surfaces in its second half, was central to its conceit: audience members were given cards as they entered the polling place, and at key moments they were asked to hold aloft cards that best represented their preference. A cast member standing silently onstage took a digital photo of the crowd, counted the signs as if they were votes, and transmitted the tally to a central website. "The musical doubled as a form of polling," said one of the producers, and his faith was not misplaced: the play correctly predicted the winner of the presidential race to within two percentage points.*

———

{It is early 2012. Like many presidents, BARACK OBAMA has aged rapidly during his first term. He looks in the mirror.}

BARACK OBAMA

Hey Michelle,
I look like hell
And now I have to get myself prepared for the campaign
From week to week
My poor physique
Bears the brunt. What an affront! How deeply inhumane.
I just turned fifty
That's only half a century
I want to free my body
From time's foul penitentiary

{BARACK OBAMA decides to get in better shape. He hires a trainer, who sets up an extensive gym and purchases large quantities of flaxseed oil.}

BARACK OBAMA

I'll go till I'm strong
Then I'll go till I'm stronger
I'll go till I cannot
Go on any longer
My pectorals will soon be acknowledged
By the nation's Electoral College

{BARACK OBAMA works out. After two weeks, the change is noticeable. After four, it is striking. Media figures, celebrities, and athletes begin to comment.}

ROGER FEDERER

I once played tennis like no man before me
I thought that nobody could equal my fitness
But have you seen President Obama lately?
He's like a Greek statue, God as my witness

MILA KUNIS

His presidency may have fizzled
But the president himself is chiseled

CHRIS MATTHEWS

He used to be skinny
Now he has muscle
I wonder if this will be
Grist for Mark Russell

{*Humorist MARK RUSSELL does, in fact, write a short song about the president's changed appearance.*}

MARK RUSSELL

Pardon me, boys
Is that the president I'm seeing?
He's bulked up so much
He looks like a different being.

{*The newly strong BARACK OBAMA, whose poll numbers have continued to slide, has an idea.*}

BARACK OBAMA

We should no longer
Hold the election
It's not a good way
To make a selection

Instead let's arm wrestle
When there's a winner, we stop
It worked like a charm
In *Over the Top*

{BARACK OBAMA signs an executive order to this effect. The Republican challengers come to Washington to try to unseat him. First, RON PAUL steps to the table. BARACK OBAMA defeats him easily.}

RON PAUL

Aiieeee! My right arm!
You shattered the limb
Is there a doctor in the house?

BARACK OBAMA

I think that you're him.

{Next comes HERMAN CAIN.}

HERMAN CAIN

You twisted my wrist
Nearly off! Holy moly!

BARACK OBAMA

Go back to Godfather's
And take the cannoli

{MICHELE BACHMANN arrives.}

MICHELE BACHMANN

Don't go easy on me
Because of my gender

BARACK OBAMA

It's easy to see
You're not a contender

{RICK SANTORUM, who is waiting in line, begins to back out of the room.}

BARACK OBAMA

Come back here, Santorum
I'll catch you and maim you
And then send you running
Back to Pennsylvania

{BARACK OBAMA goes until he has defeated all comers except the two front-runners. Finally, (GOP CANDIDATE), the former governor of (state), comes to challenge BARACK OBAMA.}

(GOP CANDIDATE)

My name is [name]
I am strong too
Stronger than others
Maybe stronger than you

I have in my hand
A speech that I wrote
It says that the country
Will sink if you float

My vision is clear
My ideas are bold
When I win, I'll deliver
The speech that I hold

BARACK OBAMA

Hey (GOP CANDIDATE),
How're things in (state), Jack?
By the time that we're done
You'll be begging to go back

A man in my position

Welcomes honest opposition
But what we have today is something worse
Since I won in '08
I've been the target of such hate
And that is something to which I'm averse

The racists
The liars
Conspiracy kooks
I've reached my limit
Put up your dukes

{(GOP CANDIDATE) and BARACK OBAMA arm wrestle. Just as OBAMA begins to push (GOP CANDIDATE)'s arm down, the scene freezes, like at the end of Rocky III. *While they are frozen, NEWT GINGRICH emerges.}*

NEWT GINGRICH

In my civilian life
When I'm not losing elections
I write popular novels
About the strange directions
That history might take
If facts were otherwise
My goal is both to teach
And also to surprise
And so we have it here
Two men but just one victory
For one it will be fruitful
For the other, valedictory
It hangs in the balance
America's fate
Will the winner be Obama
Or (GOP CANDIDATE)?

{*Behind NEWT GINGRICH, BARACK OBAMA and (GOP CAN-DIDATE) unfreeze. BARACK OBAMA is winning handily, but just before defeating (GOP CANDIDATE), he inexplicably lets up. BARACK OBAMA stands.*}

BARACK OBAMA

A veil has lifted
I've come into the light
What matters is not
My personal might
What matters is only
The strength of the nation
I'm just a symbol, the
Personification
Of a sturdy union
Of a country that works
I'm stopping the snatches
And the clean and jerks

{*BARACK OBAMA walks away from the table.*}

(GOP CANDIDATE)

Come back here now!
This is weak. This is lame.
I could have won
Or my name isn't (name)

{*BARACK OBAMA shutters up his personal gym, fires his trainer, and sells off all the extra flaxseed oil. He returns to his normal state and then goes beyond that. After about a month, he is so weak that he can only lift the Constitution.*}

BARACK OBAMA

This document is all I need

It's everything to me and mine
Forget the partisan divide
Forget walking the party line
Shame on those who turn the flag
Into a symbol of dissent
Shame on those who turn their backs
To what this country's always meant
Shame on those who preen and pose
Who propagandize and confound
We must stand for one another
We must stand on common ground

{RON PAUL, his arm in a cast, runs and tackles BARACK OBAMA and (GOP CANDIDATE). The three men fall to the floor, laughing. Secret Service men nearby also laugh. The scene freezes. NEWT GINGRICH appears again in the foreground.}

NEWT GINGRICH

My hair is whiter
Than a litter of white mice
It sits upon my head
Like I was made by Fisher-Price
I am faintly risible
A laughable figure
But I, too, agree
That the nation is bigger
Than partisan squabbling
Or one side of an issue
This makes me choke up

{BARACK OBAMA unfreezes.}

BARACK OBAMA

Here is a tissue.

CONTRIBUTORS

Jesse Adelman is a writer and musician who lives in Brooklyn, New York.

Henry Alford writes for *Vanity Fair* and *The New York Times*. His most recent book is about manners and is called *Would It Kill You to Stop Doing That?* His book about his failed acting career, *Big Kiss*, won a Thurber Prize.

Blair Becker is a slow-moving animal from the Pacific Northwest. Recent polling data suggests he is a poorly informed citizen who generally votes *yes*.

Gregory Beyer is an editor at *The Huffington Post,* and previously worked as a city reporter and occasional book reviewer at *The New York Times*. His humor writing has appeared in *The Barnes and Noble Review's Grin & Tonic*, *Whim Quarterly,* and NPR.

Matthew Bonnano has been writing humor, or some variation thereof, since his halcyon days as a columnist for his college newspaper at Shenandoah University. He now lives in New York City, where he works as a playwright some of the time and a copy editor most of the time.

Mark Brownlow is currently at work on a novel about the 1992 Black May military crackdown in Bangkok, where he lived for six years. Check it out at bangkoksblackmay .blogspot.com.

Katie Bukowski grew up in rural Wisconsin, where she was raised by parents who taught her to laugh at pretty much everything. She works in education in St. Paul, Minnesota, and spends her downtime engaged in silly conversations with her friends.

Luke Burns's work has appeared in various places on *the Internet*. He lives in New York and is busy writing more things.

Sean Carman wrote a series of dispatches about the Tunisian revolution for *McSweeney's Internet Tendency.* He has also written for *The Rumpus, The Smew,* and *Elif Batuman's Blog*. He lives in Washington, D.C.

Wyatt Cenac is a comedian who resides in New York City. While he has his own stand-up comedy album and has appeared in a few movies, he's probably best known from that show your friend's sister claims she "gets all her news from," Nickelodeon's *Fanboy & Chum Chum.*

Jimmy Chen lives in San Francisco, where he works at an office and enjoys writing. He recently started doing yoga.

Jesse Eisenberg is an Academy Award–nominated actor and playwright. Most recently, he wrote and performed in the play *Asuncion* at the Cherry Lane Theatre.

Stephen Elliott is the author of seven books, including *The Adderall Diaries*. He is the founding editor of *The Rumpus* and recently directed his first feature film, *Cherry*.

Eric Feezell is a staff writer for *The Morning News* and a contributor to *McSweeney's Internet Tendency* and *The Onion News Network*. He lives in Oakland, California, with his lovely wife and aging fat cat. You can also find him at ericfeezell.com.

Colin Perkins is a comedian and author whose writing has appeared on *Late Night with Jimmy Fallon*, *mental_floss*, *College Humor* and *Splitsider*. He is incredibly proud of his beautiful wife, Lindsey, his beautiful children, Henry and Marshall, and his beautiful talent for writing short biographies in the third person.

Caredwen Foley is an analyst for a nonprofit research organization in Cambridge, Massachusetts. She graduated from Smith College in 2009 and currently resides in Medford, Massachusetts.

Rachel Friedman is the author of *The Good Girl's Guide to Getting Lost: A Memoir of Three Continents, Two Friends, and One Unexpected Adventure*. Her work has been published in *The New York Times*, *New York* magazine, and *The Chronicle of Higher Education,* among others. She lives in Manhattan.

Mike Gallagher is an award-winning advertising creative director, writer, and *McSweeney's* contributor. Currently he is working on a screenplay. He lives in Northern California with a very supportive wife and the occasional foster dog.

Tom Gliatto is a TV critic at *People* magazine. His humor has appeared on *McSweeney's Internet Tendency* and in two *Mirth of a Nation* anthologies.

Matt Gillespie is a writer from Palatine, Illinois, currently living in San Francisco. He has published poetry in *Arsenic Lobster.*

Andrew Golden was born during the Jimmy Carter administration, but barely. He lives in Boston, Massachusetts.

Neil Graf lives in Bloomington, Indiana, with a frightening collection of ceramic rabbits. He occasionally writes poetry.

Ben Greenman is an editor at *The New Yorker* and the author of several acclaimed books of fiction, including *Superbad, Please Step Back, A Circle Is A Balloon and Compass Both,* and *Celebrity Chekhov*. He lives in Brooklyn.

Kate Hahn is an entertainment journalist and humor writer in Los Angeles. She grew up a political junkie in the Washington, D.C., suburbs and never misses *PBS News Hour*. She is the author of the short-story collection *Forgotten Fashion: An Illustrated Faux History of Outrageous Trends and Their Untimely Demise.*

Ryan Haney lives in New York City where he writes and performs comedy.

David Hart borders on stereotype, writing short comedy pieces while living in Park Slope, Brooklyn, with his wife, cat, and inhalers. He cannot grow a full beard but can be found online at davidhart.org.

Doogie Horner is the author of *Everything Explained Through Flowcharts*. He has written for *Wired,* the *London Times, Fast Company,* and *The Believer.* His comedy show *The Ministry of Secret Jokes* received a coveted Best of Philly award in 2011.

Kate Johansen was raised by a loving family in a wholesome midwestern state. But she still wound up a lawyer, lobbyist, aspiring writer, and political satirist. Go figure.

Miles Kahn is a writer, producer, and director from New York, currently working as a producer for *The Daily Show with Jon Stewart*. He has worked on numerous television shows, films, commercials, and music videos, but has resigned himself to the fact that what he'll probably be remembered for most is co-creating MTV's *Room Raiders*. He can be currently found seeking your approval on Twitter at @mileskahn.

Alex Kane is a writer for Gramps, a long-running sketch team at the Upright Citizens Brigade Theatre in New York. He can walk on his hands.

Marco Kaye was named after an island in Florida and a letter of the alphabet. His writing can be found online at *McSweeney's Internet Tendency, The Rumpus,* and *The Morning News*.

Luke Kelly-Clyne has written and performed content for *Splitsider, CollegeHumor, McSweeney's,* and *Funny or Die*. He writes for Disney's *Daily Shot with Ali Wentworth,* is a writer/producer at the New York Upright Citizen's Brigade Theatre, and performs stand-up comedy at major venues throughout New York City.

Ellie Kemper is an actress who lives in Los Angeles, California.

Dan Kennedy is author of *Loser Goes First* and *Rock On* and is a contributor to *McSweeney's*. He's working on a new novel and hosts *The Moth* podcast and StorySLAM in New York.

Lucas Klauss is a writer whose work has been featured at *McSweeney's Internet Tendency, CollegeHumor, Splitsider,* and lucasklauss.com. He also is the author of the young adult novel *Everything You Need to Survive the Apocalypse*. He lives in Brooklyn, New York.

Suzanne Kleid manages a used bookstore in San Francisco. Her work has appeared in *The Rumpus, The Believer, Bitch Magazine, We Still Like, Watchword, Pindeldyboz,* and other places. She was coeditor of *Created in Darkness by Troubled Americans: The Best of McSweeney's Humor Category,* which was released in 2004.

Gary Klien is a journalist in the San Francisco Bay Area, and the author of *The Epicurean Spy,* a novella of political humor and gastronomic excess.

Peter Krinke is an aspiring comedy writer. In his spare time, he performs stand-up for his neighbor's cats.

Rob Kutner is a writer for *Conan,* who has also written for *The Daily Show with Jon Stewart* and *Dennis Miller Live.* He is the author of *Apocalypse How: Turn the End Times into the Best of Times!* and *The Future According to Me.* And a *lot* of Supreme Court dissenting opinions, in his mind.

Mike Lacher writes and builds funny things on the Internet at mikelacher.com. His work has been featured in *McSweeney's, The New York Times Magazine, New York Magazine, wired .com, The Huffington Post,* and the *Toronto Sun.* He is the author of the book *On The Bro'd,* all of Kerouac's *On The Road* translated into bro-speak.

Nathaniel Lozier is a writer from Syracuse, New York. He is perpetually stuck between pursuing a career as a writer and the economic safety of working as an engineer.

Josh Michtom is an attorney in Hartford, Connecticut. He once had a very concise and well-written letter published in *The New York Times.*

John Moe is the author of the Pop Song Correspondences column on *McSweeney's Internet Tendency* and the book *Conservatize Me*, and has appeared in *The New York Times Magazine* and, geez, lots of other places. He lives in St. Paul, Minnesota, where he hosts various radio programs and stage events. He tried that really hot, sweaty style of yoga but found it kind of gross.

Wendy Molyneux writes for the animated show *Bob's Burgers* on Fox and is a frequent contributor to *McSweeney's Internet Tendency* and *The Rumpus*. She graduated from Pomona College and lives in Los Angeles with her husband and son. She looks terrible in hats.

Christopher Monks has been the managing editor of *McSweeney's Internet Tendency* since 2007 and is the author of the comic novel *The Ultimate Game Guide to Your Life*. He lives in Arlington, Massachusetts, with his wife and sons.

Grant Munroe's fiction and essays have appeared in *One Story, The Rumpus,* and *SMITH Magazine*. He received his MFA from New York University in 2012 and taught creative writing there as an adjunct professor. He lives in Kingsville, Ontario, and Brooklyn, New York.

Nathan Pensky writes for *Forbes* and is an associate editor for feature interviews at *PopMatters*. His fiction has been nominated for the Pushcart Prize and the Dzanc "Best of the Web" award.

Zack Poitras is a contributing writer for *The Onion* and member of the comedy group Pangea 3000. He is from Portland, Oregon, and now lives in Brooklyn.

Jamie Quatro's first story collection is forthcoming from Grove/Atlantic in spring 2013. Her work has been nominated for the Pushcart Prize and has appeared in *Tin House, Ploughshares, The Kenyon Review, Agni, Oxford American,* and elsewhere. She lives with her husband and children in Lookout Mountain, Georgia.

David Rees is a cartoonist and artisanal pencil sharpener.

Pete Reynolds grew up in the Soybean Capital of the World, a fact that most people find incredibly interesting. He lives near Washington, D.C., with his wife and two daughters. His writing tends to collect at petereynolds.tumblr.com.

Seth Reiss is the head writer at *The Onion.* He is a member of the New York–based sketch comedy group Pangea 3000.

Simon Rich's latest novel is *What in God's Name* (Little, Brown, 2012). He currently writes for Pixar.

Sarah Rosenshine lives and writes in New York City. She is a University of Chicago graduate who has contributed to *The Onion, Vice,* and other publications.

Todd Rovak is a writer living physically in New York but emotionally still in St. Louis. He believes most Rorschach inkblots show bears eating Rice Krispies treats.

Maggie Ryan Sandford is a writer/performer whose work has appeared on NPR, at ComedyCentral.com, and elsewhere. She is working on her first book.

Jim Santel is a writer from St. Louis. Educated at the Universities of Chicago and Pennsylvania, he is at work on a novel and blogs at jsantel.blogspot.com.

Sloan Schang is a writer in Portland, Oregon. He has contributed to *McSweeney's Internet Tendency, The Morning News, Outside, Wend, McSweeney's Quarterly,* and was recently a finalist for #1 Dad. Find him online at swelldone.com.

Susan Schorn is the author of the *McSweeney's* column Bitchslap. Her first book, *Smile at Strangers,* is slated for publication by Houghton-Mifflin in early 2013.

Jenny Shank's first novel, *The Ringer,* was a finalist for the Mountains and Plains Independent Booksellers Association's Reading the West Award. Her work has appeared in *Prairie Schooner, Alaska Quarterly Review, The Onion, Poets & Writers Magazine,* and *Bust Magazine.*

Mike Sacks is the author of three books: *And Here's the Kicker: Conversations with 21 Top Humor Writers*; *SEX: Our Bodies, Our Junk;* and *Your Wildest Dreams, Within Reason.*

Jim Stallard grew up in Missouri and now lives in New York City, where he is a science and humor writer. He has been a frequent contributor to *McSweeney's Internet Tendency.*

Jen Statsky is a New York–based writer and comedian. She has written for *The Onion* and *McSweeney's* and is currently a writer on *Late Night with Jimmy Fallon.*

Jonathan Stern is a film and television producer. He currently is an executive producer and writer on *Childrens Hospital, NTSF:SD:SUV:,* and *Newsreaders.* His films include *The Ten* and *Scotland, PA.* He is a contributor to *The New Yorker* and *Esquire.*

Hannah Tepper is a writer and humorist in Brooklyn, New York. Her work has been featured in *The Rumpus, McSweeney's,* and *Salon.* She enjoys mantras and Twitter (@hteps).

Alan Trotter is only twenty-nine, but he's achieved so little. More of his work can be found at greaterthanorequalto.net.

Jeremiah Tucker grew up in Joplin, Missouri. He now lives and writes in Wisconsin.

Sarah Walker is a comedian and author living in Los Angeles. Her column, Sarah Walker Shows You How, appears on *McSweeney's Internet Tendency,* and you can buy her book, *Really, You've Done Enough,* for one cent on Amazon.

Michael Ward consults on local government policy and management in New England. In his spare time, he makes really bad puns, sometimes under the Twitter handle @correspundit. He lives in Watertown, Massachusetts, with his wife.

John Warner is the author of *The Funny Man.* He's editor at large for *McSweeney's Internet Tendency* and teaches at the College of Charleston.

David Warnke is a pharmacist in St. Paul, Minnesota, when he's not masquerading as a writer of silly things.

Travis Watt writes, stands up comedically, and is more or less employed as a video game tester in Seattle. But his mind could always be changed, NASA.

Teddy Wayne is the author of the novel *Kapitoil.* The recipient of a 2011 Whiting Writers' Award and an NEA Fellowship, he was also the PEN/Robert W. Bingham Prize runner-up and a finalist for the Young Lions Fiction Award and the Dayton Literary Peace Prize. His writing appears in *The New Yorker, The New York Times,* and in his *McSweeney's* column, Teddy Wayne's Unpopular Proverbs.

Sam Weiner is a writer and performer in Los Angeles and an alumnus of Chicago's Annoyance Theatre.

Chris White is a journalist and comedian living in Washington, D.C. He once took a woman to see the cancerous growth removed from Grover Cleveland, and she still married him.

Noel Wood is an IT professional, moonlighting quizmaster, and occasional freelance writer currently living in the greater Atlanta area. He is allergic to mushrooms.

Bob Woodiwiss's (@bwsez) work appears monthly in *Cincinnati Magazine* and less reliably in several other print and online publications. He's desperate for your love and approval.